Imagine stepping back in time to an era where gladiators fought for glory, emperors wielded power with a flick of their hand, and the very streets hummed with tales of ambition, conquest, and intrigue. Welcome to the Roman Empire—a world where legends were born, empires were forged, and history was written in marble and blood. But don't worry, you won't need a toga or a chariot to explore this ancient civilization; all you need is a curious mind and a thirst for adventure.

In *The Roman Empire for Intelligent Minds: Quizzes, Stories, and Facts*, you'll find yourself at the heart of it all—debating with philosophers, strategizing with generals, and maybe even sharing a goblet of wine with Caesar himself (though, perhaps, not too close to the Ides of March). This book is your ticket to a grand tour of Rome's most thrilling moments, from the rise of Augustus to the fall of the empire, with plenty of surprises along the way.

You'll embark on this journey not just as a reader but as an active participant. Get ready to match wits with the ancients through challenging quizzes, delve into captivating stories of triumph and tragedy, and uncover the quirks and innovations that made Rome the powerhouse of the ancient world. Whether you're fascinated by Roman gods, intrigued by the legions' military might, or curious about the daily lives of citizens in the Eternal City, there's something here for everyone. So, take a deep breath, tighten your sandals, and let's march into history—Roman style!

Contents

8 Epic Acts to Understand Power, Glory, and Fall	4
Famous Roman Emperors Quiz	7
The Founding of Rome	11
Roman Military Ranks	14
Roman Phrases We Still Say Today	17
The Rise of Augustus	21
The Conquest of Gaul	25
Roman Gods and Goddesses	30
The Story of Spartacus	35
Roman Architecture	43
Cleopatra and Rome	47
The Assassination of Julius Caesar	51
Roman Mythology	55
Nero and the Great Fire of Rome	60
Famous Battles of Rome	65
The Expansion into Britain	69
Which battle am I?	74
The Building of Hadrian's Wall	77
The Reforms of Diocletian	79
Roman Daily Life	83
Roman Jokes	87

Roman Law and Governance	90
Roman Entertainment	94
Roman Literature	97
Why Do Men Think About the Roman Empire So Much?	103
The Sack of Rome by the Visigoths	106
Julius Caesar's Life and Legacy Quiz	109
The Life of Marcus Aurelius	114
The Mystery of the Lost Legion	116
The Dacian Wars	118
Roman Roads and Aqueducts	120
The Roman Senate	124
The Fall of Rome	129
Roman Religion	134
The Life of Livia Drusilla	139
The Decline and Fall of the Western Empire	141

"While we wait for life, life passes."
– Lucius Annaeus Seneca

8 Epic Acts to Understand Power, Glory, and Fall

Let's break down the Roman Empire into its essential parts, before jumping into more details and quizzes across the book.

1. The Founding Myth: Romulus, Remus, and a City of Seven Hills

The story begins with twin brothers, Romulus and Remus, who were raised by a she-wolf (yes, really!). These two had a bit of a sibling rivalry, which, like all good stories, ended in a dramatic twist—Romulus killed Remus and became the first king of Rome. And so, in 753 BC, the city of Rome was born on seven hills, destined to become the heart of an empire.

2. The Roman Republic: Where the People Ruled (Sort of)

Before emperors took the spotlight, Rome was a Republic—a government run by elected officials, or so they claimed. The Senate, a group of old, wise (and very powerful) men, made the big decisions, while the people had a say through the Assembly. This system kept things balanced until a guy named Julius Caesar decided he'd rather be a dictator. Spoiler alert: That didn't end well for him, but it paved the way for the next phase.

3. The Roman Empire: Enter the Emperors

After the Republic, Rome became an empire ruled by emperors, starting with Augustus, Caesar's grandnephew and adopted son. Augustus was the master of rebranding—he took the chaos of civil war and turned it into the Pax Romana, a 200-year period of relative peace and prosperity. The Empire stretched across Europe, North Africa, and the Middle East, with Rome at its glorious center.

4. Roman Society: Citizens, Slaves, and Gladiators

Life in Rome was all about status. At the top were the Patricians, the elite class who owned land and held power. The Plebeians were the common folk, working hard to make a living, while slaves, who made up a significant part of the population, had no rights but played crucial roles in the economy. And then there were the gladiators—slaves trained to fight in arenas for the entertainment of the masses. Think of it as the ancient version of reality TV, but with a lot more swords.

5. The Roman Military: Conquering the World, One Legion at a Time

Rome didn't become an empire by playing nice; it had one of the most disciplined and formidable armies in history. The Roman legions were the backbone of its military might, conquering lands far and wide. Their secret? Discipline, organization, and a relentless drive to expand the empire. They built roads, forts, and aqueducts as they went, leaving behind an infrastructure that still amazes us today.

6. Roman Gods and Religion: A Pantheon of Power

The Romans had a god for everything—from Jupiter, the king of the gods, to Vesta, the goddess of the hearth. Religion was deeply intertwined with daily life, politics, and even the military. Emperors were often deified after their deaths, becoming gods themselves, which was a pretty sweet retirement plan if you could get it.

7. Roman Innovations: Building an Empire, Literally

The Romans were engineers at heart, and their innovations still influence us today. They built aqueducts to bring fresh water to their cities, roads that connected the vast empire, and impressive structures like the Colosseum and the Pantheon. Their legal system, the Twelve Tables, laid the foundation for modern law. They didn't just conquer with swords—they did it with brains, too.

8. The Fall of Rome: All Good Things...

Every great empire has its downfall, and Rome was no exception. By the 5th century AD, the Western Roman Empire was crumbling under the weight of barbarian invasions, economic troubles, and internal strife. In 476 AD, the last Roman emperor was overthrown, marking the end of ancient Rome's reign. But don't worry—the Eastern Roman Empire, or Byzantine Empire, kept the flame burning for another thousand years!

So, there you have it—the Roman Empire in bite-sized pieces! We've covered the myths, the politics, the people, the gods, the conquests, and the fall. Now that you've got the basics down, you're ready to dive into the quizzes, stories, and fascinating facts that await you. Think of it as your own Roman adventure—minus the togas, but with all the excitement and knowledge to make history come alive!

Famous Roman Emperors Quiz

Match the Emperor with Their Achievements and Reign

1. This emperor is known for initiating the Pax Romana, a period of relative peace and stability across the Roman Empire. He was also the first emperor after the fall of the Roman Republic.

    a) Nero
    b) Augustus
    c) Caligula

2. He was a Stoic philosopher and the last of the Five Good Emperors. His reign was marked by military conflict and the writing of his famous work, *Meditations*.

    a) Hadrian
    b) Marcus Aurelius
    c) Trajan

3. This emperor is notorious for his tyrannical rule, his love of lavish and eccentric displays, and for reportedly "fiddling" while Rome burned.

    a) Caligula
    b) Tiberius
    c) Nero

4. Under his rule, the Roman Empire reached its greatest territorial extent, and he is known for his military conquests, particularly in Dacia.

    a) Trajan
    b) Claudius

c) Augustus

5. This emperor was known for constructing a massive wall across Britain to keep out the Picts and for his extensive travels across the empire.

   a) Hadrian
   b) Vespasian
   c) Constantine the Great

6. He was the first Roman emperor to convert to Christianity and played a pivotal role in the Edict of Milan, which granted religious tolerance throughout the empire.

   a) Diocletian
   b) Constantine the Great
   c) Septimius Severus

7. He expanded the Roman Empire through a successful campaign in Britain and is credited with the construction of the Aqua Claudia aqueduct. His reign was unexpectedly progressive given his stutter and perceived weaknesses.

   a) Augustus
   b) Claudius
   c) Nero

8. Known for his harsh economic reforms and the establishment of the Tetrarchy, this emperor aimed to stabilize the empire by dividing it into Eastern and Western halves.

   a) Diocletian
   b) Constantine the Great
   c) Trajan

Answers

1. b) Augustus

- Augustus, once known as Octavian, wasn't just the first emperor—he was the ultimate rebrander. He took a chaotic, crumbling Republic and turned it into the Roman Empire, ushering in the Pax Romana, over 200 years of peace and prosperity. Fun fact: Augustus was so revered that the month of August is named after him—because ruling an empire wasn't enough, he needed his own month too!

2. b) Marcus Aurelius

- Marcus Aurelius was the philosopher-emperor, more likely to be found pondering the meaning of life than indulging in imperial excess. His *Meditations* is still a go-to for Stoic wisdom today. Fun fact: Despite his contemplative nature, he spent much of his reign defending the empire's borders, proving that even deep thinkers can wield a sword when necessary.

3. c) Nero

- Nero is the emperor everyone loves to hate—known for his cruelty, lavish lifestyle, and that whole "fiddling while Rome burned" incident (though historians debate the accuracy of that tale). Fun fact: Nero fancied himself a great artist and performer, forcing Roman nobles to sit through his poetry and musical performances. Let's just say that back then, giving a bad review could have... deadly consequences.

4. a) Trajan

- Trajan was Rome's go-getter, expanding the empire to its greatest extent. His conquest of Dacia (modern-day Romania) brought in so much gold that it funded massive building projects, including Trajan's Column, which still stands in Rome today. Fun fact: Trajan's Column is like an ancient comic strip, spiraling upwards with scenes from his military campaigns—just with more swords and fewer capes.

5. a) Hadrian

- Hadrian was the emperor who believed in strong borders—literally. He built Hadrian's Wall across Britain to keep out those pesky Picts. He was also a bit of a globetrotter, traveling across the empire to see things firsthand. Fun fact: Hadrian was an architectural enthusiast and even had a grand villa built for himself at Tivoli, complete with a private island. Because why not?

6. b) Constantine the Great

- Constantine the Great made history as the first Roman emperor to convert to Christianity, shaping the future of the Western world. He issued the Edict of Milan, granting religious freedom and ending the persecution of Christians. Fun fact: Constantine also founded Constantinople (modern-day Istanbul), a city so pivotal that it remained the capital of the Eastern Roman Empire for over a thousand years.

7. b) Claudius

- Claudius was the underdog emperor, often underestimated due to his stutter and limp, but he ended up surprising everyone by being remarkably effective. He expanded the empire into Britain and initiated major public works. Fun fact: Claudius was so fond of scholarly pursuits that he wrote histories of the Etruscans and Carthaginians—sadly, they didn't survive, so we'll never know how he rated Hannibal's elephant skills.

8. a) Diocletian

- Diocletian was the empire's fixer, stepping in to stabilize things with some tough love—he reformed the economy, reorganized the military, and introduced the Tetrarchy, dividing the empire to make it easier to manage. Fun fact: Diocletian retired voluntarily, a rare move for an emperor. He spent his twilight years gardening, growing cabbages that were, presumably, less stressful than managing an empire.

The Founding of Rome

The Legend of Romulus and Remus

In the annals of history, few stories are as steeped in myth and intrigue as the founding of Rome. It's a tale that blends divine intervention, sibling rivalry, and the rugged determination of two brothers who were destined to build an empire. The story of Romulus and Remus isn't just the stuff of legend; it's the very bedrock upon which the Eternal City was built—a city that would one day rule the known world.

The story begins long before the twins were born, with a kingdom in turmoil. Alba Longa, an ancient city in the Latin region, was ruled by King Numitor. But as with many royal tales, there was treachery afoot. Numitor's power-hungry brother, Amulius, had other plans. In a classic villain move, Amulius overthrew Numitor, took the throne, and, to secure his hold on power, forced Numitor's daughter, Rhea Silvia, to become a Vestal Virgin. This meant she was sworn to chastity, theoretically ensuring no heirs would threaten Amulius's rule. But as you might guess, the gods had a different script in mind.

Enter Mars, the god of war, who took quite a liking to Rhea Silvia. The result of their divine union? Twin boys—Romulus and Remus. Not exactly what Amulius had planned. Panicked, Amulius ordered the infants to be drowned in the Tiber River, hoping to wash away his troubles. But the Tiber had a soft spot for the kids and deposited them safely on the riverbank. Here, they were discovered by a she-wolf, who, in one of mythology's most iconic images, suckled the twins in a cave known as the

Lupercal. The boys were later found by a shepherd, Faustulus, and his wife, who raised them as their own.

As the twins grew, so did their ambitions. Unaware of their royal lineage, they became natural leaders, protecting the shepherds and villagers from bandits. Their courage and charisma won them a loyal following. But destiny has a way of revealing itself. When they discovered their true identity and the story of their birth, the brothers didn't hesitate—they marched straight to Alba Longa, overthrew Amulius, and reinstated their grandfather, Numitor, as king. With their revenge complete, the twins were ready to forge their own path.

But where to begin? The twins decided to build a new city on the banks of the Tiber, near the very spot where they had been saved as infants. Here's where things get complicated—Romulus wanted to build on the Palatine Hill, while Remus preferred the Aventine Hill. The brothers couldn't agree, so they decided to let the gods decide through a contest of augury, the ancient practice of interpreting the will of the gods by observing the flight of birds. Romulus claimed to have seen more birds than Remus, and thus, declared himself the winner. Remus, however, wasn't convinced and mocked Romulus's new walls by jumping over them. This taunt sparked a deadly argument, and in a tragic twist of fate, Romulus killed his brother.

With Remus out of the picture, Romulus set about founding his city on April 21, 753 BC—an event celebrated as Rome's official birthday. Romulus became its first king and began establishing the city's institutions, including its military and its legal system. The city quickly grew as Romulus offered asylum to fugitives, exiles, and runaway slaves, swelling the population. However, there was one major problem: the city lacked women. To solve this, Romulus came up with a daring plan—the infamous Rape of the Sabine Women. During a festival, Romulus and his men kidnapped women from neighboring Sabine families, leading to a conflict that was eventually resolved by the women themselves, who brokered peace between the Romans and Sabines, uniting the two peoples.

Romulus ruled Rome for many years, leading it to its first victories in battle and expanding its territory. But his end was as mysterious as his beginning. According to legend, Romulus didn't die a natural death. Instead, during a thunderstorm, he vanished—some say he was taken up to the heavens by Mars, others whisper that the senators, jealous of his power, might have had a hand in his disappearance. Whatever the truth, Romulus was deified as the god Quirinus, and his legend lived on as Rome's first and greatest king.

The story of Romulus and Remus is more than just a myth; it's a symbol of Rome's strength, resilience, and destined greatness. The city they founded grew to become one of the most powerful empires in history, and their tale serves as a reminder of the complex blend of violence, divine favor, and ambition that underpinned Rome's rise. So next time you walk the ancient streets of Rome or gaze upon the ruins of the Palatine Hill, remember—it all started with a she-wolf, a river, and two brothers with a dream.

Roman Military Ranks

The Backbone of the Empire

The Roman army was one of the most formidable fighting forces in history, and much of its success was due to its strict hierarchy and discipline. From the brave soldiers on the front lines to the high-ranking officers orchestrating grand strategies, every member of the Roman military machine had a crucial role to play. The ranks within the Roman army weren't just titles—they were badges of honor, each carrying its own responsibilities, privileges, and sometimes, a healthy dose of danger.

Ready to test your knowledge on the ranks that kept Rome's legions marching forward? Let's dive into the different positions within the Roman military and see if you can identify who's who in this ancient army. Each clue will give you a glimpse into the life and duties of these soldiers. Let the battle of wits begin!

Roman Military Ranks Quiz

Identify the Ranks within the Roman Army

1. This rank was held by the backbone of the Roman legions. These soldiers made up the majority of the army and were the ones who did most of the fighting on the front lines. They were well-trained, disciplined, and could be promoted for their bravery.

    a) Centurion
    b) Legionary
    c) Tribune

2. These officers were the senior centurions of the legion, commanding around 80 to 100 men. They were known for their experience, leadership skills, and for carrying a vine staff as a symbol of their authority.

   a) Primus Pilus
   b) Centurion
   c) Optio

3. This was the highest-ranking officer in a Roman legion, typically a former senator. He commanded the entire legion, which could consist of up to 6,000 men, and was responsible for the overall strategy and operations.

   a) Legate
   b) Tribune
   c) Prefect

4. Known as the right-hand man to the centurion, this officer assisted in maintaining discipline and order within the ranks. He was often next in line to command if the centurion fell in battle.

   a) Primus Pilus
   b) Optio
   c) Decurion

Did you know? The strict discipline of the Roman army was so influential that it still impacts military practices today. For instance, the concept of "decimation"—where one in every ten soldiers was executed as punishment for the entire group's failure—originated with the Romans. While this brutal practice isn't used today, the term "decimate" has entered our everyday vocabulary, often used to describe something being reduced or destroyed significantly. The Roman approach to discipline has also influenced modern military drill procedures, where the precision and unity of movement trace back to the formations and training of Roman legions!

Answers

1. b) Legionary

- Legionaries were the core soldiers of the Roman army, making up the bulk of the legions. These professional soldiers served for 25 years and were known for their discipline and rigorous training. Fun fact: Upon retirement, they often received land or a substantial payout—talk about a well-earned pension!

2. b) Centurion

- Centurions were the backbone of the Roman command structure, each leading a century of around 80 men. They were tough, seasoned soldiers who earned their rank through years of service and bravery. Fun fact: The vine staff they carried wasn't just for show; it was used to discipline the troops when necessary.

3. a) Legate

- The Legate was the top dog in a legion, often a former senator with significant military experience. He had ultimate authority over his legion and reported directly to the emperor or a senior commander. Fun fact: The legate's command was often seen as a stepping stone to political power back in Rome.

4. b) Optio

- The Optio was the centurion's second-in-command, chosen for his loyalty and competence. He helped maintain order, manage logistics, and could take over the century if the centurion was incapacitated. Fun fact: The word "Optio" comes from the Latin word for "chosen one"—a fitting title for someone handpicked for such an important role.

Roman Phrases We Still Say Today (And Their Ancient Origins)

The Roman Empire may have crumbled centuries ago, but its influence lives on—not just in our architecture, law, and government, but also in the very words we speak. Many phrases and sayings we use today have roots in ancient Rome, proving that some things never go out of style. Let's take a look at some of these enduring expressions and their fascinating origins.

1. "Crossing the Rubicon"

In 49 BC, Julius Caesar famously crossed the Rubicon River with his army, an act of insurrection that led to a civil war. The phrase "crossing the Rubicon" has since come to mean passing the point of no return—making a decision that cannot be undone.

- **Usage Today:** Whether it's quitting your job or making a bold move in a relationship, when someone "crosses the Rubicon," they've made a choice that changes everything.

2. "Carpe Diem"

Latin for "Seize the day," this phrase comes from the Roman poet Horace. In his work *Odes*, Horace urged readers to make the most of the present rather than relying too much on the future.

- **Usage Today:** You'll hear this one tossed around in everything from graduation speeches to Instagram captions. It's the ultimate YOLO (You Only Live Once) of ancient Rome, reminding us all to live life to the fullest.

3. "Et tu, Brute?"

These are the famous last words attributed to Julius Caesar in Shakespeare's play *Julius Caesar* as he is being assassinated by his friend Brutus. The phrase, though possibly fictional, has come to symbolize the ultimate betrayal by a friend.

- **Usage Today:** Anytime someone feels stabbed in the back by a close friend or ally, you might hear them sarcastically mutter, "Et tu, Brute?" It's a shorthand way of expressing that bitter sting of betrayal.

4. "All Roads Lead to Rome"

In ancient Rome, the saying "all roads lead to Rome" was literal—Roman roads were constructed to radiate outwards from the capital, making it the center of the known world.

- **Usage Today:** Nowadays, this phrase means that different methods or actions will eventually lead to the same result. It's a reminder that there are many ways to achieve a goal.

5. "Beware the Ides of March"

The "Ides of March" refers to March 15th on the Roman calendar. It's most famous as the day Julius Caesar was assassinated in 44 BC. The phrase comes from a soothsayer's warning in Shakespeare's *Julius Caesar*.

- **Usage Today:** While people don't necessarily use this phrase literally anymore, it's often referenced in a tongue-in-cheek way to warn someone about an impending bad day or when trouble might be brewing.

6. "Veni, Vidi, Vici"

Julius Caesar coined this phrase, meaning "I came, I saw, I conquered," after a swift victory in the Battle of Zela in 47 BC. It's the ultimate expression of confident, decisive success.

- **Usage Today:** This phrase is perfect for celebrating a big win, whether it's acing a test, crushing a presentation, or completing a daunting task with ease. It's a classic boast with a Roman twist.

7. "When in Rome, Do as the Romans Do"

This saying has its roots in the advice given by St. Ambrose, a 4th-century Roman bishop, who suggested that when visiting Rome, it's best to follow the customs of the locals.

- **Usage Today:** This is the go-to phrase for adapting to new environments. Whether you're traveling abroad or just visiting a friend's house, it's a reminder to respect local customs and blend in.

8. "Fortune Favors the Bold"

The phrase "Fortes fortuna adiuvat," or "Fortune favors the bold," was used by the Roman playwright Terence. It's also attributed to Pliny the Elder, who supposedly said it just before sailing into the eruption of Mount Vesuvius.

- **Usage Today:** You'll hear this one when someone's about to take a big risk. It's a way of encouraging bravery and suggesting that those who dare to take chances are more likely to succeed.

9. "In Vino Veritas"

This Latin phrase means "In wine, there is truth." It comes from the belief that people are more likely to speak their true thoughts and feelings after a few drinks, an idea that was as popular in ancient Rome as it is now.

- **Usage Today:** It's often used in a light-hearted way to suggest that alcohol can loosen tongues, revealing what people really think or feel, sometimes with humorous or awkward consequences.

10. "Divide and Conquer"

The strategy of "divide et impera" (divide and rule) was used by Julius Caesar and other Roman leaders to keep control over their territories by fostering divisions among their enemies.

- **Usage Today:** This phrase is used in both politics and business, often in a more metaphorical sense. It's a strategy for weakening opposition by breaking it up into smaller, less powerful groups.

From conquering empires to navigating modern life, these phrases show just how much the legacy of Rome still influences the way we think, speak, and act today. The Romans may be long gone, but their words—and their wisdom—continue to resonate.

The Rise of Augustus

Trivia Journey Through the Birth of the Empire

Welcome to an exciting trivia adventure that will take you through the dramatic transformation of a young, ambitious leader named Octavian into the revered Augustus, the first emperor of Rome. Get ready to test your knowledge, uncover fascinating facts, and enjoy a bit of Roman wit along the way. Let's dive in!

1. Octavian's Early Days

- *Let's start with an easy one to warm you up.*

At the tender age of 19, Octavian was thrust into the world of Roman politics and power struggles. Who was his famous great-uncle and adoptive father, whose assassination in 44 BC set the stage for Octavian's rise to power?

    a) Julius Caesar
    b) Marcus Antonius (Mark Antony)
    c) Cicero

2. The Battle for Power

- *Time to kick it up a notch!*

After Caesar's death, Octavian found himself in a bitter struggle for control of Rome. Which famous naval battle in 31 BC marked the decisive victory for Octavian over his rival, Mark Antony, and Cleopatra?

    a) Battle of Philippi
    b) Battle of Actium
    c) Battle of Zama

3. The First Among Equals

- *Let's see how well you know your Roman titles.*

In 27 BC, after solidifying his power, Octavian was given a new title by the Senate, marking the beginning of the Roman Empire. What was this title, which also became the name by which he is famously known?

    a) Imperator
    b) Princeps
    c) Augustus

4. The Clever Reforms

- *Now, for a little dive into the details.*

Augustus was not just a military leader but also a savvy politician who knew how to win over the people and the Senate. Which reform did Augustus introduce to reorganize Rome's military forces, ensuring the loyalty of the legions to him personally?

    a) The establishment of the Praetorian Guard
    b) The creation of the Roman Navy
    c) The division of Rome into administrative regions

5. Augustus's Propaganda Machine

- *Getting a bit tougher now!*

Augustus was a master of image-making and used various means to shape public perception. Which famous monument, commissioned by Augustus, celebrated his victory at Actium and symbolized the peace and prosperity of his reign?

    a) Ara Pacis (Altar of Peace)
    b) Circus Maximus
    c) Pantheon

6. Family Ties and Succession

- *You're doing great—let's see how deep your knowledge goes.*

Augustus's rule was marked by concerns over succession, as he had no sons. Which of these individuals was NOT considered as a potential heir to Augustus's throne?

- a) Marcellus, his nephew
- b) Tiberius, his stepson
- c) Julius Caesar, his brother

7. The Lasting Legacy

- *For the final challenge, a question on Augustus's enduring impact.*

Augustus's reign ushered in a period of relative peace and stability across the Roman Empire, lasting for over 200 years. What is the name of this era, often regarded as the golden age of Rome?

- a) Pax Romana
- b) Pax Augustus
- c) Roman Renaissance

Answers

1. a) Julius Caesar

- That's right! Julius Caesar was not just a dictator but also Octavian's great-uncle and adoptive father. His assassination led to a power vacuum that young Octavian would eventually fill—by any means necessary.

2. b) Battle of Actium

- Indeed, the Battle of Actium was the turning point where Octavian's forces defeated those of Mark Antony and Cleopatra. This victory paved the way for Octavian to become the undisputed ruler of Rome.

3. c) Augustus

- Octavian was awarded the title "Augustus" by the Senate, a name meaning "revered" or "venerable." It was a title that signaled a new era for Rome—no longer a Republic, but an Empire under Augustus's rule.

4. a) The establishment of the Praetorian Guard

- Augustus cleverly formed the Praetorian Guard, an elite unit of soldiers tasked with protecting him. This move not only ensured his safety but also kept the military's loyalty firmly in his hands.

5. a) Ara Pacis (Altar of Peace)

- The Ara Pacis was a masterpiece of Augustan propaganda, celebrating his victory and the ensuing peace. The richly decorated altar was both a religious site and a political statement, embodying the peace Augustus claimed to bring.

6. c) Julius Caesar, his brother

- Gotcha! Julius Caesar wasn't Augustus's brother—he was his great-uncle and adoptive father. Marcellus and Tiberius were indeed considered as potential heirs, with Tiberius eventually succeeding Augustus as emperor.

7. a) Pax Romana

- Congratulations, you've reached the end! The Pax Romana, or "Roman Peace," was a remarkable period of stability that Augustus's reign helped initiate. It's remembered as one of the greatest achievements of his leadership.

The Conquest of Gaul

Julius Caesar's Campaigns and Their Impact on Roman Expansion

Julius Caesar's conquest of Gaul is one of the most famous military campaigns in history, not only for its sheer scale and success but also for its profound impact on the expansion and future of the Roman Empire. This series of campaigns, which took place between 58 BC and 50 BC, saw Caesar bring vast territories under Roman control, dramatically altering the political and cultural landscape of Western Europe. The conquest of Gaul wasn't just about expanding borders; it was about securing Caesar's place in history and setting the stage for the end of the Roman Republic.

Gaul, a region roughly corresponding to modern-day France, Belgium, Luxembourg, and parts of Switzerland, Germany, and Italy, was a patchwork of tribal societies. These tribes were independent, often warring with one another, and seen by the Romans as barbarians. However, they were far from disorganized; they had their own systems of governance, warrior classes, and alliances. Julius Caesar, then a Roman general and governor of the Roman provinces in Gaul, saw an opportunity to not only secure Rome's northern borders but also to boost his own political career.

The catalyst for Caesar's campaign was a migration crisis. The Helvetii, a Celtic tribe from what is now Switzerland, began migrating westward, threatening the stability of Roman territories. Caesar responded by decisively defeating them at the Battle of Bibracte in 58 BC. This victory not only stopped the Helvetii but also marked the beginning of Caesar's long and brutal conquest of Gaul. Over the next few years, Caesar methodically subdued the Gallic tribes, employing a combination of military brilliance, political manipulation, and sheer ruthlessness.

One of Caesar's most significant achievements during the conquest was the defeat of the Germanic leader Ariovistus, who had been invited by some Gallic tribes as a protector but had quickly become a tyrant. By driving Ariovistus back across the Rhine, Caesar not only eliminated a threat to Roman authority but also sent a powerful message to the Gallic tribes: Rome was the dominant power, and resistance was futile. This victory further solidified Caesar's reputation as a military genius and paved the way for further Roman expansion.

However, the conquest of Gaul was far from straightforward. The Gallic tribes, though often fragmented, were capable of uniting against a common enemy. The most famous of these resistances was led by Vercingetorix, a chieftain of the Arverni tribe. In 52 BC, Vercingetorix managed to unite several tribes in a last-ditch effort to drive the Romans out of Gaul. The ensuing conflict culminated in the Siege of Alesia, one of Caesar's most remarkable military achievements. Despite being outnumbered and surrounded, Caesar's forces built massive fortifications around Alesia, trapping Vercingetorix inside and defeating the Gallic relief forces. The fall of Alesia effectively ended organized resistance in Gaul, and Vercingetorix was captured and later executed in Rome.

The impact of Caesar's conquest of Gaul was enormous. Militarily, it extended Rome's territory to the English Channel and the Rhine River, providing a buffer against potential threats from Germanic tribes. Economically, the conquest brought vast wealth to Rome in the form of spoils, slaves, and new trading opportunities. The integration of Gaul into the Roman world also led to the spread of Roman culture, language, and infrastructure, laying the foundations for the Romanization of Western Europe.

Politically, the conquest of Gaul had profound consequences for Rome itself. Caesar's success made him immensely popular with the Roman people but also alarmed the Senate, who feared his growing power and ambition. The wealth and loyalty of the legions that Caesar had gained from his Gallic campaigns gave him the resources and influence to challenge the authority of the Senate, ultimately leading to the civil war between Caesar and Pompey. The victory in this civil war would end the Roman Republic and usher in the era of the Roman Empire, with Caesar's adopted heir, Augustus, becoming the first emperor.

Julius Caesar's campaigns in Gaul were more than a series of battles; they were the crucible in which the fate of the Roman Republic was forged. The legacy of these campaigns can still be seen today, not just in the borders of modern Europe but in the enduring influence of Roman culture and governance.

Ten Crazy Facts About Julius Caesar

1. Caesar the Fashion Icon

- Julius Caesar was not just a military genius; he was also a trendsetter. He was known for wearing a laurel wreath, not just as a symbol of victory, but also to cover his thinning hair. Caesar's distinctive style influenced Roman fashion, and wearing a laurel wreath became a symbol of status in Rome.

2. Kidnapped by Pirates—And Laughed About It

- At the age of 25, Julius Caesar was captured by Cilician pirates. When they demanded a ransom of 20 talents of silver, Caesar insisted they ask for 50, because he believed he was worth more. He also told the pirates he would have them crucified once freed—and after the ransom was paid, he did exactly that.

3. The Calendar Reformer

- Before Caesar's time, the Roman calendar was a mess, with politicians manipulating it for their own gain. Caesar reformed the calendar in 46 BC, creating the Julian calendar, which introduced the 365-day year and the leap year. This calendar was so effective that it remained in use in parts of Europe until 1582 and is still the basis for the calendar we use today.

4. Caesar's Love Life Was Legendary

- Caesar was known for his numerous romantic liaisons, but his most famous affair was with Cleopatra, the queen of Egypt. The two had a son, Caesarion, and their relationship was as much about politics as passion. Cleopatra even visited Rome and stayed in Caesar's villa, which caused quite a scandal in the city.

5. He Was Declared Dictator for Life

- After his many military victories, Caesar was declared dictator perpetuo (dictator for life) in 44 BC. This unprecedented move alarmed many in the Senate, as it essentially made him a king in all but name—anathema to the Roman Republic, which prided itself on avoiding monarchy.

6. Caesar Had Epilepsy

- Historical accounts suggest that Caesar suffered from epilepsy, a condition that was not well understood at the time. Despite this, he remained physically and mentally strong, leading campaigns and managing the complexities of Roman politics. Some historians believe his condition may have influenced his decision-making and leadership style.

7. The Origin of "Caesarean" Section

- Although Julius Caesar wasn't born by what we now call a Caesarean section, the procedure's name is often mistakenly attributed to him. In fact, the term comes from the Latin word *caesus*, meaning "cut," and was used because the procedure involved cutting into the abdomen. The legend that Caesar himself was born this way is likely a myth.

8. Crossing the Rubicon—The Point of No Return

- When Caesar crossed the Rubicon River in 49 BC, he uttered the famous phrase *alea iacta est* ("the die is cast"), signaling the start of a civil war. By doing so, he violated Roman law, which prohibited generals from bringing armies into Italy, effectively declaring war on the Senate and sealing his fate as a revolutionary.

9. A Master of Propaganda

- Caesar was a skilled writer and used his talents to shape his public image. His commentaries on the Gallic Wars, *De Bello Gallico*, were not just military reports but carefully crafted pieces of propaganda. They were written in a clear, direct style that made them accessible to the Roman public, bolstering his reputation as a brilliant commander.

10. His Assassination Was Foreshadowed by Omens

- Caesar's assassination on the Ides of March (March 15, 44 BC) was preceded by a series of ominous signs, according to ancient sources. A soothsayer famously warned Caesar to "beware the Ides of March." On the day of his assassination, his wife, Calpurnia, had a nightmare in which she saw him bleeding to death, but Caesar dismissed the warning and went to the Senate, where he was stabbed 23 times by conspirators.

Roman Gods and Goddesses

Who Am I? Quiz with a Pop Culture Twist

Let's match the Roman deities with their domains, but with a fun twist! Each clue will not only describe the god or goddess but might also include a pop culture reference that connects to their myth. Ready to play?

1. I am the king of the gods, ruling the heavens with my mighty thunderbolt. My Roman name is associated with a planet, and my Greek counterpart is Zeus. If you've seen Disney's *Hercules*, you might recall my Greek version giving some fatherly advice.

Who am I?

- a) Mars
- b) Jupiter
- c) Saturn

2. I am the goddess of love and beauty, often depicted with a dove or a seashell. If you've heard the phrase "Venus in Furs" from the song by The Velvet Underground or seen Botticelli's *The Birth of Venus*, you know who I am. My Greek counterpart is Aphrodite.

Who am I?

- a) Minerva
- b) Venus
- c) Diana

3. I am the god of war, feared and revered by soldiers. You've seen my influence if you've ever played a game from the *God of War* series, where my Greek counterpart, Ares, causes chaos.

Who am I?

- a) Vulcan
- b) Neptune
- c) Mars

4. I am the goddess of wisdom, war strategy, and the arts. My symbol is the owl, and if you're a fan of *Harry Potter*, you'll remember the wisdom of Hermione, who embodies many of my traits. My Greek counterpart is Athena.

Who am I?

- a) Vesta
- b) Minerva
- c) Juno

5. I am the god of the sea, controlling the waves and storms with my trident. Remember Aquaman from DC Comics? My Greek counterpart, Poseidon, wields similar power in mythology.

Who am I?

- a) Neptune
- b) Apollo
- c) Bacchus

6. I am the messenger of the gods, known for my winged sandals and helmet. I guide souls to the underworld and protect travelers, merchants, and thieves. If you've watched the *Flash* TV series, you'll recognize some similarities between my speed and that of the Scarlet Speedster. My Greek counterpart is Hermes.

Who am I?

- a) Mercury
- b) Janus
- c) Vulcan

7. I am the goddess of the hunt, the wilderness, and the moon. My bow and arrows are always ready. If you've seen *The Hunger Games*, think of me as the original Katniss Everdeen. My Greek counterpart is Artemis.

Who am I?

   a) Ceres
   b) Diana
   c) Venus

8. I am the god of the underworld, ruling over the dead. My domain is dark and mysterious. Remember the chilling portrayal of my Greek counterpart, Hades, in Disney's *Hercules*? That's me, but in Roman form.

Who am I?

   a) Pluto
   b) Mars
   c) Vulcan

9. I am the goddess of the hearth, home, and family. My flame burns eternally, symbolizing the heart of Roman life. You might see a touch of my influence in the nurturing, protective nature of Mrs. Weasley in *Harry Potter*. My Greek counterpart is Hestia.

Who am I?

   a) Vesta
   b) Juno
   c) Minerva

10. I am the god of wine, revelry, and ecstasy. I inspire both joy and madness. Think of me as the ancient party god—sort of like the wildest rock star, but with more divine flair. My Greek counterpart is Dionysus.

Who am I?

   a) Apollo
   b) Bacchus

c) Saturn

Answers

1. b) Jupiter

- Jupiter is the king of the Roman gods, wielding thunderbolts and ruling the heavens. If you've seen Disney's *Hercules*, you've met his Greek counterpart, Zeus, giving some solid advice to his son.

2. b) Venus

- Venus is the goddess of love and beauty, and if you've heard "Venus in Furs" or seen Botticelli's iconic painting, you've seen her influence. She's the Roman counterpart of Aphrodite.

3. c) Mars

- Mars, the god of war, inspired fear and respect, much like Ares, his Greek counterpart, whom you might know from the *God of War* video games.

4. b) Minerva

- Minerva, the goddess of wisdom, has a connection to the owl, a symbol of wisdom you'll recognize if you've read *Harry Potter*. She's the Roman version of Athena.

5. a) Neptune

- Neptune, the Roman god of the sea, is like a mythological version of Aquaman's Poseidon. He rules the waters with a trident.

6. a) Mercury

- Mercury, the swift-footed messenger of the gods, has a speed that rivals the Flash's! His Greek counterpart is Hermes.

7. b) Diana

- Diana, goddess of the hunt and moon, would be right at home in *The Hunger Games* as the original Katniss Everdeen. Her Greek counterpart is Artemis.

8. a) Pluto

- Pluto is the Roman god of the underworld, much like the fiery Hades from Disney's *Hercules*. He rules over the dead with a dark and mysterious presence.

9. a) Vesta

- Vesta, the goddess of the hearth, is the Roman counterpart to Hestia. Her eternal flame represents the warmth and protection found in homes—something Mrs. Weasley would definitely appreciate!

10. b) Bacchus

- Bacchus, the god of wine and revelry, would have fit right in with any rock star of today. He's the life of the ancient party, much like his Greek counterpart, Dionysus.

The Story of Spartacus

A Tale of Rebellion and Freedom

In the annals of history, few stories capture the imagination as vividly as that of Spartacus, the gladiator who dared to defy the might of Rome. Born into slavery, Spartacus became a symbol of resistance against oppression, leading one of the most significant slave revolts in the ancient world. His story is one of courage, struggle, and the relentless pursuit of freedom, even in the face of impossible odds.

Spartacus's early life is shrouded in mystery, but what we do know is that he was born in Thrace, a region in the Balkans, and was likely a warrior before being captured and sold into slavery by the Romans. Like many slaves, Spartacus was condemned to the brutal life of a gladiator, trained to fight and kill for the entertainment of Roman crowds. The conditions were harsh, the survival rate grim, and for many, the arena was a death sentence. But Spartacus was different—he was a natural leader, and he had no intention of dying for the amusement of his captors.

In 73 BC, Spartacus and about 70 fellow gladiators decided they had endured enough. Armed with kitchen utensils and makeshift weapons, they fought their way out of the gladiator school in Capua and fled to the nearby slopes of Mount Vesuvius. It was there, among the volcanic cliffs, that Spartacus's rebellion began in earnest. As word of the revolt spread, slaves from across the region flocked to his banner. What started as a small band of escapees quickly grew into a formidable army, united by their common desire for freedom.

Spartacus proved to be a brilliant strategist. His forces, though largely untrained and poorly equipped, managed to outmaneuver and defeat several Roman legions sent to crush the rebellion. His army swelled to tens of thousands as more slaves joined the cause, driven by the hope that they might finally break free from their chains. Spartacus's victories were not just military successes; they were symbolic blows against the very foundation of Roman society, which was built on the backs of slaves.

For two years, Spartacus led his followers through Italy, defeating Roman forces time and again. He dreamed of leading his army across the Alps to freedom in their homelands, but as the rebellion grew, so did the ambitions of those within it. Many of his followers wanted to stay in Italy, plundering the riches of the Roman countryside. Torn between his desire for freedom and the practicalities of leading such a large, diverse force, Spartacus eventually turned south, aiming to reach the coast and possibly escape to Sicily.

However, the tide began to turn against Spartacus and his followers. The Roman Senate, alarmed by the scale of the rebellion, put the seasoned general Marcus Licinius Crassus in charge of crushing the revolt. Crassus was one of the wealthiest men in Rome, and he spared no expense in raising a massive army to hunt down Spartacus. Knowing that time was running out, Spartacus attempted to negotiate with pirates to secure passage for his army to Sicily, but the deal fell through, leaving him and his followers trapped in southern Italy.

The final confrontation came in 71 BC, on the plains of Lucania, near the river Silarus. Spartacus, knowing that the end was near, reportedly killed his own horse before the battle, declaring that if he won, he would have plenty of Roman horses to choose from, and if he lost, he would no longer need one. In a desperate and valiant fight, Spartacus and his army fought with everything they had, but they were no match for the disciplined legions of Crassus. Spartacus was killed in the battle, and the rebellion was crushed.

In the aftermath, Rome exacted a brutal revenge. Over 6,000 captured slaves were crucified along the Appian Way, the road leading to Rome, as a grim warning to any who might consider rebellion. The body of Spartacus was never found, and he became a martyr, his legacy living on as a symbol of resistance against tyranny and oppression.

The story of Spartacus is more than just a tale of rebellion; it is a testament to the human spirit's unyielding desire for freedom. Despite the odds, Spartacus dared to challenge the most powerful empire in the world, inspiring countless others to dream of a life beyond servitude. His story has been told and retold through the ages, a reminder that even in the darkest of times, the light of hope and the quest for freedom can never be fully extinguished.

Did You Know? The Story Behind the Colosseum's Construction

Did you know that the Colosseum, Rome's most iconic structure, was built on the site of a grand lake that once belonged to Emperor Nero's lavish palace, the Domus Aurea? After Nero's death, Emperor Vespasian decided to give the land back to the people by constructing a massive amphitheater for public spectacles—a move that was as political as it was practical.

Did you know that construction of the Colosseum began in AD 72 under Vespasian and was completed in AD 80 by his son, Emperor Titus? It took just eight years to build this architectural marvel, an astonishing feat considering the size and complexity of the structure. The inauguration was celebrated with 100 days of games, including gladiatorial combats, animal hunts, and even mock naval battles.

Did you know that the Colosseum's design was revolutionary for its time? It could hold between 50,000 to 80,000 spectators, who entered through 80 arched entrances, ensuring that the massive crowds could be seated quickly and efficiently. The tiered seating was a reflection of Roman society, with the best seats reserved for the elite and the nosebleeds for the commoners.

Did you know that the Colosseum featured a complex system of elevators and trapdoors beneath the arena floor? These allowed for dramatic entrances of gladiators, wild animals, and stage sets, turning the games into theatrical spectacles. The hypogeum, the underground network of tunnels and chambers, was a masterpiece of engineering that added an element of surprise and danger to the events.

Did you know that the Colosseum was originally known as the Flavian Amphitheatre, named after the Flavian dynasty that commissioned its construction? The name "Colosseum" was later derived from a colossal statue of Nero that once stood nearby. Though the statue is long gone, the name stuck and has become synonymous with the arena itself.

Did you know that the Colosseum was built using over 100,000 cubic meters of travertine stone, held together not by mortar, but by iron clamps weighing tons? This innovative technique gave the Colosseum its enduring strength, allowing it to withstand earthquakes, fires, and the passage of nearly two millennia.

Did you know that the Colosseum was also equipped with a massive retractable awning, known as the *velarium*, to protect spectators from the sun? Operated by a team of sailors, this giant canvas could be extended or retracted depending on the weather, providing shade and comfort to the crowd below.

Did you know that after the fall of the Roman Empire, the Colosseum fell into disrepair and was even used as a quarry for building materials? Many of the stones that once formed the Colosseum were repurposed for the construction of churches and palaces throughout Rome, contributing to the city's evolving landscape.

Did you know that despite its bloody history as a site of gladiatorial combat, the Colosseum is now a symbol of peace? Each Good Friday, the Pope leads a torchlit "Way of the Cross" procession around the amphitheater, and the Colosseum is illuminated in gold whenever a death sentence is commuted or a country abolishes the death penalty.

Did you know that the Colosseum remains one of the most visited landmarks in the world, attracting millions of tourists each year? Even after nearly 2,000 years, the grandeur and history of this ancient arena continue to captivate the imagination, making it a testament to the enduring legacy of Roman engineering and culture.

The Roman Republic vs. The Roman Empire: True or False Quiz

Let's test your knowledge about the key differences and events that shaped the transition from the Roman Republic to the Roman Empire. Each statement will challenge your understanding of this pivotal period in history. Ready to separate fact from fiction? Let's go!

1. **True or False:** The Roman Republic was characterized by a complex system of checks and balances, with power divided between the Senate, the Consuls, and the Assembly.

2. **True or False:** Julius Caesar's crossing of the Rubicon River marked the beginning of the Roman Empire.

3. **True or False:** During the Roman Republic, the title of "emperor" was regularly used to describe the highest-ranking official in Rome.

4. **True or False:** The assassination of Julius Caesar in 44 BC was a pivotal event that led directly to the fall of the Roman Republic.

5. **True or False:** The Roman Empire officially began when Octavian was given the title "Augustus" by the Senate in 27 BC, marking the end of the Republic.

6. **True or False:** The Roman Republic relied heavily on a citizen army, while the Roman Empire increasingly used professional soldiers, including non-Roman mercenaries.

7. **True or False:** The Senate retained its power throughout the Roman Empire, continuing to make all major decisions regarding governance and military action.
8. **True or False:** The Pax Romana, a period of relative peace and stability, occurred during the Roman Republic.
9. **True or False:** The Roman Republic's political system included two consuls who were elected annually, whereas the Roman Empire was typically ruled by a single emperor with virtually unlimited power.
10. **True or False:** The Roman Empire's expansion was significantly larger than that of the Roman Republic, extending from Britain to Egypt at its peak.

Did you know? The transition from the Roman Republic to the Roman Empire was so significant that it inspired the modern concept of "crossing the Rubicon," which means making an irreversible decision. When Julius Caesar crossed the Rubicon River in 49 BC, he famously declared, *alea iacta est* ("the die is cast"), knowing that this bold move would lead to civil war and change Rome forever. Today, the phrase is used in everything from business to pop culture to describe taking a decisive, often risky action with no turning back!

Answers

1. True

- The Roman Republic was indeed characterized by a system of checks and balances. Power was divided between the Senate, the Consuls, and the Assembly, creating a complex political structure intended to prevent any one individual from gaining too much control.

2. False

- Julius Caesar's crossing of the Rubicon in 49 BC marked the beginning of a civil war, but it did not mark the start of the Roman Empire. The Roman Empire began later, in 27 BC, when Octavian (Augustus) was declared the first emperor.

3. False

- During the Roman Republic, the title of "emperor" did not exist. The highest-ranking officials were the consuls, who were elected annually. The title "emperor" became prominent only after the establishment of the Roman Empire.

4. True

- The assassination of Julius Caesar was indeed a critical event that led to the end of the Roman Republic. His death plunged Rome into a series of civil wars, eventually leading to the rise of Augustus and the beginning of the Roman Empire.

5. True

- The Roman Empire officially began in 27 BC when the Senate awarded Octavian the title "Augustus." This marked the end of the Roman Republic and the beginning of the Empire.

6. True

- The Roman Republic relied on a citizen army composed of land-owning men. In contrast, the Roman Empire increasingly relied on a professional army, which included non-Roman mercenaries and soldiers recruited from the provinces.

7. False

- While the Senate continued to exist during the Roman Empire, its power was significantly reduced. The emperor held the ultimate authority, and the Senate's role became largely advisory.

8. False

- The Pax Romana, a period of relative peace and stability, occurred during the Roman Empire, not the Republic. It began with the reign of Augustus and lasted for about 200 years.

9. True

- The Roman Republic's political system included two consuls who shared power and were elected annually. In contrast, the Roman Empire was typically ruled by a single emperor with almost absolute power.

10. True

- The Roman Empire's expansion was indeed much larger than that of the Roman Republic. At its height, the Empire stretched from Britain in the northwest to Egypt in the southeast, covering a vast and diverse territory.

Roman Architecture

Identify Famous Landmarks

Let's see how well you know your Roman landmarks! Each clue will describe a famous Roman structure, with hints that connect them to something you might recognize in modern-day life. Ready to test your architectural knowledge?

1. This massive amphitheater is an ancient version of your favorite sports stadium, designed to host epic gladiatorial games, mock naval battles, and public spectacles. Its oval shape and tiered seating allowed up to 80,000 spectators to cheer on the action. Think of it as Rome's version of a modern-day Super Bowl arena.
What is it?

2. This temple was originally dedicated to all the gods of ancient Rome. Its dome, which still holds the record for the world's largest unreinforced concrete dome, has a central opening called the oculus, allowing light (and rain) to pour in. If you've ever admired a domed building like the U.S. Capitol or St. Peter's Basilica, you've seen its influence.
What is it?

3. This engineering marvel was designed to bring fresh water to Roman cities from distant sources. Picture a modern-day water pipeline, but with elegant arches and stonework. It's a testament to Roman ingenuity, and remnants of it can still be seen across Europe today.
What is it?

4. This public square in the heart of ancient Rome was the center of political, commercial, and social life—imagine it as the Times Square of its day, bustling with activity, debates,

and gatherings. It was surrounded by important government buildings, temples, and markets.
What is it?

5. This grand structure was built by the Emperor Hadrian as a tomb for himself and his family. Over time, it was repurposed as a fortress and even a papal residence. Today, it's known for its massive circular shape and connection to a famous Roman bridge, making it a striking monument on the Roman skyline.
What is it?

6. This triumphal arch was constructed to commemorate a significant military victory. You can think of it as an ancient version of a victory parade, but in stone form! It's covered in detailed carvings depicting the victorious campaigns of the emperor it was built for. Many cities around the world, including Paris with its Arc de Triomphe, have been inspired by this type of monument.
What is it?

7. This enormous racecourse was the home of Rome's famous chariot races, capable of holding up to 250,000 spectators. Picture it as the ancient equivalent of a NASCAR or Formula 1 track, but with horses and chariots instead of cars. The site is now a public park, but the shape of the track is still visible.
What is it?

Answers

1. The Colosseum

Answer: *The Colosseum*

- Think of the Colosseum as ancient Rome's version of the ultimate sports arena—only instead of touchdowns, the crowds cheered for gladiators and wild animals. Here's a crazy fact: The Colosseum could even be flooded for mock naval battles, where they staged entire war scenes on water. Take that, halftime shows!

2. The Pantheon

Answer: *The Pantheon*

- The Pantheon is like the original "open-concept" building—literally! Its massive dome has a 30-foot-wide hole (the oculus) at the top, which lets in sunlight and, occasionally, rain. And get this: the dome was such an engineering marvel that it held the record for the largest in the world for over 1,300 years. Beat that, modern architects!

3. The Aqueducts

Answer: *The Aqueducts*

- Roman aqueducts were like the Wi-Fi of ancient Rome—essential infrastructure that everyone relied on but often took for granted. These stone marvels could transport water over dozens of miles using gravity alone. Crazy fact: The longest Roman aqueduct stretched over 250 miles! That's like having a water pipeline from New York to Boston, without a single pump.

4. The Roman Forum

Answer: *The Roman Forum*

- The Roman Forum was the original "it" place—where deals were struck, laws were debated, and gossip spread faster than a modern-day tweet. Picture it as Rome's answer to Wall Street, Capitol Hill, and your local farmer's market, all rolled into one. Fun tidbit: Julius Caesar once gave a speech here that was so persuasive, it's said he could have sold sand in the Sahara!

5. Castel Sant'Angelo

Answer: *Castel Sant'Angelo*

- Castel Sant'Angelo started as Emperor Hadrian's ultra-luxury tomb and later became a fortress, a papal palace, and even a prison. It's basically Rome's version of a Swiss Army knife—handy for all occasions! Fun fact: There's a secret passage connecting the castle to the Vatican, perfect for a quick escape when things got a little too hot in the papal kitchen.

6. The Arch of Titus

Answer: *The Arch of Titus*

- The Arch of Titus is like the ultimate victory selfie, captured in stone. This triumphal arch was built to commemorate Emperor Titus's victory in the Siege of Jerusalem. And here's a crazy fact: The arch features a carving of the Menorah from the Jewish temple, which Titus's army looted. It's probably the earliest example of an ancient "flex."

7. The Circus Maximus

Answer: *The Circus Maximus*

- The Circus Maximus was the place to be for a high-octane, edge-of-your-seat chariot race, with up to 250,000 fans screaming for their favorite team—imagine NASCAR meets the Kentucky Derby, but with way more toga parties. And here's something wild: Chariot teams were as popular as today's sports teams, with die-hard fans and even merch. Team Red or Team Green, anyone?

Cleopatra and Rome

The Political and Romantic Entanglements Between Egypt and Rome

The story of Cleopatra VII, the last queen of Egypt, is one of the most captivating tales in ancient history. It's a saga of political maneuvering, romantic entanglements, and the epic clash of two powerful civilizations—Egypt and Rome. Cleopatra's relationships with Julius Caesar and Mark Antony not only shaped the fate of Egypt but also played a significant role in the eventual rise of the Roman Empire. Her life was a delicate dance of power and passion, where the personal and the political were inextricably linked.

Cleopatra and Julius Caesar: The Alliance of Power

Cleopatra's first major entanglement with Rome began with Julius Caesar. In 48 BC, Cleopatra found herself in a precarious position. She was embroiled in a bitter civil war with her brother, Ptolemy XIII, for the throne of Egypt. Enter Julius Caesar, the Roman general who had just arrived in Egypt while pursuing his own enemy, Pompey. Seeing an opportunity, Cleopatra had herself smuggled into Caesar's quarters, famously rolled up in a carpet. This bold move impressed Caesar, who was captivated by her intelligence, charm, and political acumen.

The partnership between Cleopatra and Caesar was mutually beneficial. Caesar, who was at the peak of his power, needed Egypt's wealth to fund his ambitions in Rome, while Cleopatra needed Caesar's military might to secure her throne. Their alliance was cemented not only by political necessity but also by a romantic relationship that resulted in a son, Ptolemy XV, known as Caesarion. Cleopatra's position was solidified when Caesar defeated Ptolemy XIII's forces and installed her as the sole ruler of Egypt. For a time, Egypt and Rome enjoyed a symbiotic relationship, with Cleopatra visiting Rome and living in Caesar's villa, much to the scandal of the Roman elite.

Cleopatra and Mark Antony: The Love That Shook the World

Cleopatra's second entanglement with Rome was even more dramatic, involving Mark Antony, one of Caesar's most trusted generals. After Caesar's assassination in 44 BC, Rome was thrown into chaos, with power struggles between various factions. Mark Antony emerged as one of the most powerful men in Rome, sharing control with Octavian (later Augustus) and Lepidus in the Second Triumvirate.

In 41 BC, Antony summoned Cleopatra to Tarsus (modern-day Turkey) to explain her loyalty during the recent Roman civil war. Cleopatra, ever the master strategist, arrived on a golden barge dressed as Aphrodite, the goddess of love, which enchanted Antony. What began as a political meeting quickly turned into a legendary romance. Antony and Cleopatra became inseparable, with Antony spending more and more time in Alexandria, Cleopatra's capital. Their relationship scandalized Rome, as Antony seemed to be abandoning his Roman duties in favor of the exotic and wealthy queen of Egypt.

Their union wasn't just about love; it was also about power. Antony and Cleopatra formed a powerful alliance against Octavian, who was positioning himself as the sole ruler of Rome. Antony even declared Cleopatra's son, Caesarion, as Julius Caesar's legitimate heir, directly challenging Octavian's claim. In 32 BC, the Roman Senate declared war on Cleopatra, framing it as a foreign conflict rather than a civil war.

The Battle of Actium: The Fall of Antony and Cleopatra

The conflict between Rome and Egypt culminated in the Battle of Actium in 31 BC, one of the most significant naval battles in history. Octavian's forces, led by his brilliant general Agrippa, faced off against the combined fleets of Antony and Cleopatra. The battle ended in disaster for Antony and Cleopatra; their fleet was destroyed, and they were forced to flee back to Egypt.

Back in Alexandria, with Octavian's forces closing in, both Antony and Cleopatra faced the grim reality of their defeat. Antony, believing Cleopatra to be dead, fell on his sword. Cleopatra, determined to avoid the humiliation of being paraded through Rome as a captive, famously took her own life, allegedly by allowing an asp (a venomous snake) to bite her.

The Legacy of Cleopatra and Rome

The deaths of Antony and Cleopatra marked the end of the Ptolemaic dynasty and the beginning of a new era for Rome. Egypt became a province of the Roman Empire, and Octavian, now Augustus, became the first Roman emperor. Cleopatra's dream of an independent, powerful Egypt ended with her death, but her legacy as one of history's most fascinating and influential figures endures.

Cleopatra's entanglements with Rome weren't just a series of love affairs; they were strategic alliances that shaped the course of history. Her ability to navigate the treacherous waters of Roman politics and use her personal relationships to further her political goals is a testament to her intelligence and ambition. Though her life ended in tragedy, Cleopatra's story continues to captivate, reminding us of the complex interplay between power, politics, and passion in the ancient world.

4 Crazy Facts About Cleopatra and Rome

1. Cleopatra's Luxury Barge

Cleopatra's famous meeting with Mark Antony on the luxurious barge wasn't just a romantic gesture—it was a calculated power move. The barge was adorned with purple sails and silver oars, and the air was filled with the scent of incense. Cleopatra knew how to make an entrance, using every sense to seduce and impress Antony. The scene was so grand that Shakespeare later immortalized it in *Antony and Cleopatra.*

2. The Hidden Message in Cleopatra's Death

While Cleopatra's death by asp is the most famous version, some historians believe she may have used poison instead. The asp story was likely promoted to symbolize Cleopatra as a dangerous and exotic ruler—Rome's final conquest over a deadly and seductive enemy.

3. Antony and Cleopatra's Secret Wine Club

Cleopatra and Antony were known for their extravagant parties, but they also founded a drinking society called the "Inimitable Livers." The club was famous for its lavish feasts, wine-drinking contests, and wild entertainment, where the two lovers celebrated their power and wealth with friends and allies. It's ancient Rome's version of an exclusive VIP club!

4. Cleopatra's 'Son of Caesar'

Cleopatra named her son Caesarion, claiming he was the rightful heir of Julius Caesar. However, his existence was a direct threat to Octavian, who declared Caesarion as "the last pharaoh" and had him executed to secure his rule. Some even speculate that Caesarion escaped and lived in hiding, a mystery that adds to Cleopatra's legendary status.

The Assassination of Julius Caesar

The Conspiracy and Aftermath

Julius Caesar's assassination on the Ides of March, 44 BC, remains one of the most infamous events in history—a dramatic culmination of political intrigue, personal betrayal, and the complex dynamics of power in ancient Rome. The conspiracy that led to his death was driven by a group of senators who believed they were saving the Republic from tyranny. But was Caesar's death justified? Shakespeare's portrayal in *Julius Caesar* suggests that Caesar's ambition and potential for tyranny warranted his demise. Let's explore this argument by examining Caesar's physical weaknesses, his hunger for power, and the potential dangers he posed to Rome.

Physical Weaknesses: A Vulnerable Leader

In *Julius Caesar*, Shakespeare subtly highlights Caesar's physical vulnerabilities. Historically, Caesar was known to suffer from epilepsy, which was seen as a sign of weakness in a leader who needed to command respect and authority. In the play, Caesar's physical ailments are used to symbolize his vulnerability and the fragility of his power. For example, during the Lupercal festival, Caesar faints in public, an episode that underscores his human frailty and contrasts sharply with his image as an invincible ruler.

Shakespeare presents these weaknesses not just as a personal flaw but as a potential liability for Rome. A leader perceived as weak or compromised might be seen as an easy target for Rome's enemies, both internal and external. This perception could undermine the stability of the state, making Caesar's physical limitations a critical factor in the justification for his assassination.

Power-Hungry and Egotistical: The Seeds of Tyranny

Perhaps the most compelling argument for Caesar's assassination lies in his unquenchable thirst for power. In both history and Shakespeare's play, Caesar is depicted as increasingly autocratic, seeking to consolidate power at the expense of the Republic's traditional values. His acceptance of honors and titles, such as "dictator for life," alarmed many senators who feared that Caesar aimed to become a king in all but name—a direct violation of Rome's longstanding aversion to monarchy.

In *Julius Caesar*, Shakespeare portrays Caesar as a man blinded by his own ambition and ego. His famous refusal of the crown during the Lupercal festival, while ostensibly an act of humility, is depicted as a calculated move to gauge public opinion. This scene suggests that Caesar was not only power-hungry but also deeply manipulative, willing to play the political game to achieve his ends.

Caesar's disregard for the Republic's traditions and his apparent desire to concentrate power in his own hands made him a threat to the ideals of Roman liberty. The conspirators, led by Brutus and Cassius, believed that by killing Caesar, they were preventing the rise of a tyrant who would destroy the Republic's democratic foundations.

A Danger to Rome: The Potential for Destruction

The most significant concern among Caesar's opponents was the belief that his rule would ultimately harm Rome more than it would help. Shakespeare's *Julius Caesar* reflects this fear, portraying Caesar as a leader whose ambition outweighed his judgment and whose ego blinded him to the consequences of his actions. The conspirators feared that Caesar's unchecked power would lead to the erosion of the Senate's authority, the rise of a dictatorial regime, and the eventual collapse of the Republic.

In the play, Brutus justifies the assassination by arguing that it was necessary to protect Rome from the potential tyranny of Caesar's rule.

He famously states, "Not that I loved Caesar less, but that I loved Rome more." This line encapsulates the moral dilemma faced by the conspirators: they did not kill Caesar out of personal hatred but out of a perceived duty to safeguard the Republic.

However, the aftermath of Caesar's assassination proved that their actions, while intended to protect Rome, instead plunged it into chaos. The power vacuum left by Caesar's death led to a brutal civil war, the rise of Augustus (Caesar's adopted heir), and the eventual transformation of the Republic into the Roman Empire—a turn of events that ironically fulfilled the very fate the conspirators sought to avoid.

Did Caesar Deserve to Die? Shakespeare?

Whether Julius Caesar deserved to die is a question that has been debated for centuries, and Shakespeare's portrayal adds layers of complexity to the discussion. Caesar's physical weaknesses, his insatiable ambition, and the potential dangers he posed to Rome certainly provide a strong case for the justification of his assassination. Yet, the chaos that followed his death also raises questions about whether the conspirators truly served the Republic or simply accelerated its demise.

In the end, Caesar's assassination can be seen as both a necessary act of preservation and a tragic mistake. It is a testament to the dangers of absolute power and the perils of political idealism, where the line between heroism and betrayal becomes dangerously blurred.

1. Caesar Was Warned Multiple Times

Julius Caesar received numerous warnings about the plot against him, including a famous one from a soothsayer who told him to "beware the Ides of March." Even his wife, Calpurnia, had a nightmare about his death and begged him to stay home that day, but Caesar dismissed these warnings and went to the Senate, sealing his fate.

2. The Assassination Was a Group Effort

Caesar was stabbed 23 times by as many as 60 conspirators, all senators who had sworn an oath to protect the Republic. Despite the large number of attackers, only one wound—delivered by Brutus—was fatal. The sheer number of participants in the assassination shows the extent of the conspiracy and the collective fear of Caesar's power.

3. Caesar's Famous Last Words Might Be Fiction

According to Shakespeare, Caesar's last words were "Et tu, Brute?" ("And you, Brutus?"), expressing his shock at Brutus's betrayal. However, historians like Suetonius claim Caesar said nothing as he died, while others suggest he uttered the Greek phrase "Kai su, teknon?" ("You too, my child?"). The dramatic last words might be more literary invention than historical fact.

4. Caesar's Death Led to the Rise of the Roman Empire

Ironically, Caesar's assassination, meant to save the Republic, instead paved the way for its end. The resulting civil wars eventually led to the rise of Caesar's adopted heir, Octavian (later Augustus), who became the first emperor of Rome. The Republic the conspirators tried to protect was replaced by the Roman Empire, which would dominate the Mediterranean world for centuries.

Roman Mythology

Match Myths and Legends to Their Roman Counterparts

Let's see how well you know Roman mythology! Below, I'll describe famous myths and legends. Your challenge is to match each one with its Roman counterpart. Ready to put your mythological knowledge to the test?

1. This legendary hero completed twelve nearly impossible labors, including slaying the Nemean Lion and capturing the Golden Hind. Known for his incredible strength, he's the ultimate hero in both Greek and Roman mythology.

Who is his Roman counterpart?

- a) Hercules
- b) Aeneas
- c) Odysseus

2. This legendary founder of Rome was raised by a she-wolf alongside his twin brother. His tale is central to Roman identity, and he's known for building the city that would become the heart of the Roman Empire.

Who is he?

- a) Romulus
- b) Theseus
- c) Perseus

3. This cunning and clever hero devised the idea of the Trojan Horse, leading to the fall of Troy. Afterward, he embarked on a long and perilous journey home, filled with encounters with mythical creatures.

Who is the Roman version of this Greek hero?

a) Aeneas
b) Odysseus
c) Ulysses

4. This tragic love story involves a queen of Carthage who falls in love with a Trojan hero. However, their love ends in sorrow when the hero leaves to fulfill his destiny, and the queen, heartbroken, takes her own life.

What is the name of the Trojan hero in Roman mythology?

a) Paris
b) Achilles
c) Aeneas

5. This goddess was the twin sister of Apollo and was associated with the hunt, wild animals, and the moon. She is often depicted carrying a bow and arrows.

Who is she in Roman mythology?

a) Diana
b) Minerva
c) Juno

6. This powerful god ruled the underworld and was associated with death and the afterlife. He was known to abduct the goddess of spring to be his queen.

Who is this Roman god?

a) Hades
b) Pluto
c) Mars

7. This god of the sea wielded a trident and controlled all bodies of water. He was known for his temper and his rivalry with other gods.

Who is he in Roman mythology?

- a) Neptune
- b) Poseidon
- c) Vulcan

8. This myth involves a pair of star-crossed lovers whose secret meetings led to a tragic misunderstanding and their untimely deaths. Their story inspired one of Shakespeare's most famous plays.

Who are these lovers in Roman mythology?

- a) Pyramus and Thisbe
- b) Orpheus and Eurydice
- c) Paris and Helen

9. This god of war was known for his fierce nature and was often depicted in armor, ready for battle. He was the son of Jupiter and Juno, and his Greek counterpart was Ares.

Who is he?

- a) Apollo
- b) Mars
- c) Mercury

10. This tale features a great craftsman who built wings for himself and his son to escape from Crete. The son, in his youthful arrogance, flew too close to the sun, leading to a tragic end.

What is the name of the son in Roman mythology?

- a) Icarus
- b) Phaethon
- c) Daedalus

Answers

1. a) Hercules

- *Hercules* is the Roman counterpart of the Greek hero Heracles. Known for his incredible strength and his twelve labors, he remains one of the most celebrated figures in Roman mythology.

2. a) Romulus

- *Romulus* is the legendary founder of Rome, raised by a she-wolf with his twin brother, Remus. His story is central to Roman identity and mythology.

3. c) Ulysses

- *Ulysses* is the Roman version of Odysseus, the clever hero who came up with the idea of the Trojan Horse and embarked on a long journey home, facing countless trials.

4. c) Aeneas

- *Aeneas* is the Trojan hero who falls in love with Dido, the queen of Carthage. Their tragic love story is a key part of Roman mythology, particularly in Virgil's *Aeneid*.

5. a) Diana

- *Diana* is the Roman goddess of the hunt and the moon, the twin sister of Apollo, and the equivalent of the Greek goddess Artemis.

6. b) Pluto

- *Pluto* is the Roman god of the underworld, the equivalent of the Greek Hades. He is associated with death and the afterlife and abducted Proserpina (Persephone) to be his queen.

7. a) Neptune

- *Neptune* is the Roman god of the sea, wielding a trident and controlling the oceans. He is the counterpart of the Greek god Poseidon.

8. a) Pyramus and Thisbe

- *Pyramus and Thisbe* are the tragic lovers in Roman mythology whose story of forbidden love and a tragic end inspired Shakespeare's *Romeo and Juliet*.

9. b) Mars

- *Mars* is the Roman god of war, known for his aggressive nature and often depicted in full armor. He is the Roman counterpart of the Greek god Ares.

10. a) Icarus

- *Icarus* is the son of Daedalus who flew too close to the sun, causing his wax wings to melt and leading to his tragic fall—a tale of hubris and youthful recklessness in Roman mythology.

Nero and the Great Fire of Rome

The Infamous Emperor and the Mysterious Blaze

The Great Fire of Rome, which occurred in AD 64, is one of the most infamous events in Roman history. The blaze ravaged the city for over a week, destroying much of its infrastructure and leaving thousands homeless. But what makes this disaster even more significant is the role of Emperor Nero, whose reputation has been forever linked with the fire. Over the centuries, stories of Nero's actions during and after the fire have fueled speculation, conspiracy theories, and enduring legends. Was Nero truly responsible for the devastation, or was he simply a convenient scapegoat? Let's explore the event and the man behind it.

The Great Fire: A City in Flames

On the night of July 18, AD 64, a fire broke out in the densely populated area of Rome known as the Circus Maximus, a hub of commerce and entertainment. Fanned by strong winds and fed by the wooden structures that dominated the city, the fire quickly spread, engulfing homes, shops, and temples. Ancient Rome, with its narrow streets and close-packed buildings, was especially vulnerable to such a disaster, and within hours, the fire was raging out of control.

For six days, the fire raged across Rome, eventually consuming ten of the city's fourteen districts. Three districts were completely destroyed, and only four remained untouched. The city, once the heart of the vast Roman Empire, was left in ruins. The devastation was unprecedented, and the people of Rome were desperate for answers and someone to blame.

Nero: The Infamous Emperor

Nero, who became emperor at the age of 16, was already a controversial figure by the time of the fire. His rule was marked by extravagance, artistic ambitions, and accusations of tyranny. Known for his love of music, theater, and grandiose public works, Nero was often viewed by the Roman elite as a self-indulgent ruler who cared more for his personal pleasures than for the responsibilities of the empire. His reputation was further tarnished by his involvement in the deaths of his mother, Agrippina the Younger, and his first wife, Claudia Octavia.

As the fire ravaged Rome, Nero was not in the city but at his villa in Antium, approximately 35 miles away. According to the historian Tacitus, Nero returned to Rome as soon as he heard the news and personally led relief efforts. He opened his palaces to shelter the homeless and arranged for food supplies to be distributed at no cost. Despite these efforts, rumors quickly spread that Nero had either started the fire himself or had done little to stop it.

The Myth of Nero "Fiddling" While Rome Burned

One of the most enduring images of the Great Fire of Rome is that of Nero "fiddling" while the city burned. This story, which paints Nero as a callous and indifferent ruler, is likely a myth. The fiddle, or violin, did not exist at the time; instead, Nero was known to play the lyre, an ancient stringed instrument. The origins of this tale may lie in Nero's love of music and his reputation for performing in public. Some accounts suggest that Nero sang the "Sack of Ilium" (the fall of Troy) while watching the city burn, a scene that would have been seen as both inappropriate and highly symbolic of Rome's destruction.

Whether or not Nero actually played music during the fire, the story served to cement his image as a tyrant disconnected from the suffering of his people. The idea that he would treat such a catastrophic event as a mere performance only fueled public anger and suspicion.

Blaming the Christians: A Convenient Scapegoat

As public discontent grew, Nero needed a scapegoat to deflect blame from himself. He found it in the fledgling Christian community of Rome. At this time, Christians were a small and somewhat mysterious religious group, often viewed with suspicion by the Roman populace. Nero accused the Christians of starting the fire and unleashed a brutal persecution against them. According to Tacitus, Christians were arrested, tortured, and executed in horrific ways—some were covered in animal skins and torn apart by dogs, while others were set alight to serve as human torches in Nero's gardens.

Nero's persecution of Christians was one of the earliest and most severe in Roman history, and it marked the beginning of a long period of hostility between the Roman state and the Christian faith. The act of blaming the Christians for the fire served Nero's immediate political needs, but it also created a narrative that would resonate throughout history, particularly in the context of the later Christianization of the Roman Empire.

Rebuilding Rome: Nero's Grand Ambitions

In the aftermath of the fire, Nero embarked on an ambitious project to rebuild Rome. He used the opportunity to redesign the city with wider streets, improved fireproofing measures, and more open spaces. The most controversial aspect of this reconstruction was the construction of his new palace, the Domus Aurea, or "Golden House." This sprawling complex, with its opulent gardens, artificial lake, and grand architecture, was seen by many as a testament to Nero's vanity and a symbol of his disregard for the suffering caused by the fire.

The Domus Aurea covered a vast area in the heart of Rome, including land that had been cleared by the fire. For many Romans, the sight of Nero's golden palace rising from the ashes of their city was proof that the emperor had either started the fire to make way for his palace or had at least taken advantage of the disaster to further his own interests.

Nero's Legacy: Tyrant or Misunderstood?

Nero's reign ended in AD 68, four years after the Great Fire, when he was declared a public enemy by the Senate and forced to commit suicide. His death marked the end of the Julio-Claudian dynasty, and his legacy has been the subject of debate ever since. Was Nero truly the monster that history remembers, or was he a complex ruler who became the victim of propaganda and political machinations?

The Great Fire of Rome remains one of the most significant events of Nero's reign and a key factor in his historical reputation. While the true cause of the fire may never be known, the stories that emerged from it have shaped the way we view Nero and his legacy. Whether he was a tyrant who played music while Rome burned or a ruler who did his best to manage an unprecedented disaster, Nero's connection to the fire is a testament to the power of narrative in shaping history.

1. Nero's Golden Palace: A Palace Fit for a Megalomaniac

The Domus Aurea, Nero's extravagant palace, was so vast and luxurious that it included a 120-foot-tall statue of Nero himself, known as the Colossus of Nero. This statue later inspired the name of the Colosseum, which was built near the site of the Golden House.

2. The Lyre, Not the Fiddle

Despite the famous saying, Nero didn't actually fiddle while Rome burned—he played the lyre. The fiddle didn't exist in Nero's time, making the story more metaphorical than factual. However, Nero's musical performances were legendary, and he even competed in Greek musical contests (where he conveniently never lost).

3. Nero's Extreme Makeover: Rome Edition

After the fire, Nero took charge of Rome's reconstruction, implementing new building codes with fireproof materials. Despite the disaster, some of the innovations he introduced helped improve the city's infrastructure, showing that even Nero's darkest moments had silver linings.

4. A Modern-Day Villain?

Nero's image as a villain persisted long after his death. In fact, some early Christians believed Nero was the Antichrist, and his name became synonymous with evil in later Christian writings. His reputation was so bad that even centuries later, people referred to particularly cruel rulers as "Neroes."

Famous Battles of Rome

Trivia Journey Through Rome's Greatest Conflicts

Ready to dive into the epic world of Roman warfare? These battles weren't just clashes of armies; they were turning points that shaped the course of history. Each question will challenge you to identify a famous Roman battle based on intriguing clues about tactics, outcomes, and the drama that unfolded on the battlefield. The difficulty ramps up as you go, so buckle up your sandals, and let's march into the fray!

1. Let's Start Easy: The Ambush in the Forest

Imagine you're deep in the dense, misty forests of Germania. The Roman legions, used to the open fields, are marching in long columns through unfamiliar territory when suddenly, all hell breaks loose. Ambushed by Germanic tribes, the Romans are caught off guard and suffer a devastating defeat. This battle was a shocking loss for Rome and is often considered one of its greatest military disasters.

Can you name this infamous battle?

- a) Battle of Cannae
- b) Battle of Teutoburg Forest
- c) Battle of Zama

2. A Clash of Giants: Elephants and Legions

Now, picture a dusty plain in North Africa. On one side, the disciplined Roman legions; on the other, an army led by one of history's greatest military tacticians, who famously crossed the Alps with war elephants. This battle ended a long and brutal war between Rome and a powerful rival state. It's remembered as a brilliant display of Roman strategy, where the Romans used their enemy's strengths against them.

Which battle is this?

a) Battle of Zama
b) Battle of Pharsalus
c) Battle of Actium

3. Turning the Tide: A Sea Battle with Lasting Consequences

Get ready to set sail! Imagine fleets of ships clashing on the sparkling waters of the Mediterranean. On one side is a Roman general vying for control of the entire Republic; on the other, a rival general and his famous Egyptian ally. The outcome of this naval battle would decide the fate of Rome and mark the end of the Republic, paving the way for an empire.

What is this decisive battle?

a) Battle of Mylae
b) Battle of Actium
c) Battle of Cannae

4. The Bloodbath in Southern Italy

Now, let's talk about one of the bloodiest days in Roman military history. You're in Southern Italy, facing a Carthaginian general who has already given Rome a run for its money. He's outnumbered but uses brilliant tactics to encircle and annihilate a massive Roman army. This battle is still studied in military academies today as a masterpiece of double envelopment.

Can you name this devastating defeat for Rome?

a) Battle of Teutoburg Forest
b) Battle of Cannae
c) Battle of Philippi

5. A Final Stand in Greece

We're in Greece now, facing the remnants of the forces loyal to a famous Roman general who met his end on the Ides of March. The forces of the assassins are crushed by the combined might of their opponents, leading to the rise of the Second Triumvirate and the eventual fall of the Roman Republic. This battle was not just the end of a military campaign but the end of an era.

Which battle was it?

a) Battle of Philippi
b) Battle of Zama
c) Battle of Actium

6. The Fall of a City: A Siege for the Ages

Our final question takes us to a city under siege. The city's defenders, known for their discipline and valor, face overwhelming odds as the Roman legions surround them. The siege lasts for months, and when the city finally falls, it marks the end of a bitter and destructive conflict between Rome and its former allies. The fall of this city shocked the ancient world and demonstrated Rome's ruthless determination to crush all resistance.

Which siege am I describing?

a) Siege of Alesia
b) Siege of Syracuse
c) Siege of Carthage

Answers

1. b) Battle of Teutoburg Forest

- The Battle of Teutoburg Forest was a catastrophic defeat for Rome in AD 9, where three Roman legions were ambushed and destroyed by Germanic tribes. This loss had a profound impact on Roman expansion plans in Germania, and the region remained outside Roman control.

2. a) Battle of Zama

- The Battle of Zama in 202 BC was the decisive confrontation between Rome, led by Scipio Africanus, and Carthage, led by Hannibal. Scipio's clever tactics, including neutralizing

Hannibal's war elephants, led to a Roman victory, ending the Second Punic War.

3. b) Battle of Actium

- The Battle of Actium in 31 BC was a crucial naval battle where Octavian's fleet defeated the combined forces of Mark Antony and Cleopatra. This victory gave Octavian control over Rome and led to the establishment of the Roman Empire.

4. b) Battle of Cannae

- The Battle of Cannae in 216 BC was one of Rome's darkest hours. Hannibal's Carthaginian forces encircled and annihilated a much larger Roman army, inflicting one of the most devastating defeats in Roman history. The battle is famous for its strategic brilliance.

5. a) Battle of Philippi

- The Battle of Philippi in 42 BC was fought between the forces of Mark Antony and Octavian against the armies of Julius Caesar's assassins, Brutus and Cassius. The defeat of Brutus and Cassius marked the end of the Roman Republic and the rise of the Empire.

6. c) Siege of Carthage

- The Siege of Carthage in 146 BC marked the end of the Third Punic War. After a brutal and lengthy siege, Rome finally destroyed the city, effectively wiping Carthage off the map and establishing Rome's dominance in the Mediterranean.

The Expansion into Britain

Rome's Conquest and Control of Britannia

The story of Rome's expansion into Britain is a tale of ambition, conquest, and the relentless drive of the Roman Empire to extend its borders to the farthest corners of the known world. Britannia, a mysterious and remote island to the Romans, represented both a challenge and an opportunity. The Roman conquest of Britain began in AD 43 under Emperor Claudius and spanned several decades, leaving an indelible mark on the island's history and culture.

The Roman Invasion: Claudius's Bold Gamble

Before the Romans, Britain was a land of warring tribes, rich in resources but largely disconnected from the Mediterranean world. Julius Caesar had attempted to invade Britain in 55 and 54 BC, but his campaigns were more exploratory than conquest-driven. It wasn't until nearly a century later, under Emperor Claudius, that Rome launched a full-scale invasion of the island.

In AD 43, Claudius, seeking to bolster his political standing and secure a lasting legacy, ordered the invasion of Britain. The Roman legions, led by General Aulus Plautius, landed on the shores of southeast England, near the modern-day city of Kent. Despite fierce resistance from the local tribes, particularly the Catuvellauni under the leadership of King Caratacus, the Romans quickly established a foothold. Claudius himself arrived later with reinforcements, including war elephants, to demonstrate Rome's might. The sight of these massive creatures, previously unknown to the Britons, likely had a profound psychological impact on the defenders.

Within months, the Romans had captured Camulodunum (modern-day Colchester), which became the first Roman capital of Britannia. Claudius's campaign was a success, and he returned to Rome to celebrate a triumph, cementing his reputation as a conqueror.

The Romanization of Britain

After the initial conquest, Rome set about the long process of Romanizing Britain. This involved building roads, establishing military forts, and founding Roman-style towns. Londinium (London), Eboracum (York), and Verulamium (St Albans) are just a few of the settlements that began as Roman outposts and grew into thriving urban centers.

The Romans introduced new agricultural practices, engineering marvels such as aqueducts, and a complex road network that facilitated the movement of troops and trade across the island. The famous Roman baths, temples, and villas dotted the landscape, blending Roman culture with local traditions.

However, the process of Romanization was met with resistance. The indigenous tribes, proud and fiercely independent, frequently rebelled against Roman rule. The most famous of these uprisings was led by Boudica, queen of the Iceni tribe, in AD 60-61. Enraged by the mistreatment of her people and the seizure of her lands, Boudica led a revolt that saw several Roman settlements, including Londinium, burned to the ground. Despite initial successes, her rebellion was eventually crushed by the Roman governor Suetonius Paulinus, and Roman control was reasserted.

Hadrian's Wall: Rome's Northern Frontier

The northern part of Britain, home to the fierce Picts and other tribes, proved particularly difficult to conquer. In AD 122, Emperor Hadrian visited Britain and ordered the construction of a massive wall to mark the northern boundary of Roman control. Hadrian's Wall stretched for 73 miles across the width of northern England, from the

River Tyne in the east to the Solway Firth in the west. It was more than just a defensive structure; it was a symbol of Rome's power and the boundary between the civilized world and the barbarian lands beyond.

The wall was heavily fortified with garrisons, forts, and milecastles (small fortlets) that housed Roman soldiers tasked with defending the frontier and controlling trade and movement across the border. Despite this formidable barrier, the northern tribes continued to pose a threat, leading to the construction of the Antonine Wall further north, though this was eventually abandoned in favor of Hadrian's more defensible position.

The Decline of Roman Britain

For nearly four centuries, Rome maintained control over Britain, but the empire's grip began to weaken in the late 4th century. As Rome faced increasing pressures from barbarian invasions on the continent and internal political instability, its ability to defend distant provinces like Britain diminished. In AD 410, the Roman Emperor Honorius famously instructed the Britons to look to their own defenses, effectively signaling the end of Roman rule in Britain.

The departure of the Roman legions left a power vacuum that would lead to the fragmentation of Roman Britain into smaller, independent kingdoms. The Roman infrastructure, laws, and culture left a lasting legacy on Britain, but the island would soon enter a new era marked by the arrival of the Anglo-Saxons and the decline of Roman influence.

Legacy of the Roman Conquest

The Roman conquest and occupation of Britain fundamentally altered the course of the island's history. The Romans introduced new technologies, architecture, and governance that would shape British society for centuries to come. Even after the Romans left, their influence persisted in the form of roads, cities, and the Latin language, which would later form the basis for many English words.

The story of Rome's expansion into Britain is not just a tale of conquest but also one of cultural exchange, adaptation, and resilience. It highlights the complexities of empire-building and the lasting impact that such endeavors can have on the conquered lands.

1. Elephants on British Soil

When Emperor Claudius arrived in Britain to secure his victory, he brought with him war elephants—an astonishing sight for the native Britons who had never seen such creatures before. The elephants were not just for battle; they served as a psychological weapon, demonstrating Rome's overwhelming power and technological superiority.

2. Londinium: A City Built on Marshes

Modern-day London, or Londinium as the Romans called it, was founded around AD 47-50 on marshy land along the River Thames. The Romans built the city from scratch, constructing roads, a bridge across the Thames, and a port that would become one of the most important trade hubs in the Roman Empire.

3. Boudica's Revenge

Boudica, queen of the Iceni, led a fierce revolt against Roman rule that resulted in the destruction of several Roman cities, including Londinium. It's estimated that her forces killed as many as 80,000 Romans and pro-Roman Britons before her defeat. Her uprising remains one of the most famous acts of resistance against the Roman Empire.

4. Hadrian's Wall Wasn't Just a Wall

Hadrian's Wall wasn't simply a barrier; it was a complex frontier system that included a ditch, a military road, and watchtowers. The wall housed an estimated 15,000 soldiers who patrolled and protected the border from Pictish raids. Soldiers stationed there came from all over the Roman Empire, making it a melting pot of cultures.

5. The Mystery of the Roman Ninth Legion

The Roman Ninth Legion, one of Rome's most famous military units, mysteriously disappeared from historical records after being stationed in Britain. Some historians believe it was wiped out during a rebellion in northern Britain, while others think it was transferred to another part of the empire. Its fate remains one of the great mysteries of Roman history.

6. Roman Roads: The Original Highways

The Romans constructed over 2,000 miles of roads in Britain, many of which formed the basis of the country's modern road network. These roads were built with remarkable precision, featuring layers of materials for drainage and durability, and were so well-constructed that some are still in use today, nearly 2,000 years later!

Which battle am I?

Identify the Battle Based on Clues

Question 1:

I was one of Rome's worst nightmares—literally. Imagine waking up to find an enemy general staring down at you from the Alps on an elephant (yes, an elephant). My opponent pulled off one of the greatest ambushes in military history, utterly humiliating the Romans with a double envelopment maneuver. After this, the Romans avoided big open battles with me, and who could blame them? The year was 216 BC, and my name still makes Roman soldiers shudder.

Which battle am I?

Question 2:

Rome's back was against the wall—quite literally, as my battle took place in the shadow of the capital. My opponent was a Germanic giant who had already sacked the Eternal City once. But this time, Rome fought back, and with a little help from a plague and starvation, we managed to send him packing. In 452 AD, I helped preserve what was left of the crumbling empire, and my enemy's nickname? "The Scourge of God."

Which battle am I?

Question 3:

It was a battle of endurance, and Rome had to get creative. When your city is besieged for over two years, you start to think outside the box—how about building a second wall around the enemy's siege wall? Genius, right? In 70 AD, this battle wasn't just about military might; it was about crushing a rebellion and making an example of the last holdout of resistance. Spoiler alert: The temple didn't survive.

Which battle am I?

Question 4:

This one's for the underdog lovers. I faced an army twice my size, but no sweat—my legionaries were known for discipline, not numbers. My opponent, the king of Pontus, thought he could outsmart us with waves of cavalry and archers, but he didn't count on the Roman testudo (turtle) formation. Afterward, I wrote a famously short dispatch to the Senate: "I came, I saw, I conquered." Casual, right? The year was 47 BC.

Which battle am I?

Question 5:

I'm the battle where Rome hit rock bottom—and I mean bottom. Three entire legions lost, and an entire forest swallowed them up. Imagine fighting in unfamiliar, dense woods with no room to maneuver. My enemy knew the terrain, and he had a bone to pick with Rome, having learned their tactics as one of their own. In 9 AD, the Romans walked into a trap that would haunt them for centuries. The Rhine became Rome's limit after this.

Which battle am I?

Answers

1. Battle of Cannae (216 BC)

- Hannibal's famous double envelopment of the Roman army at Cannae during the Second Punic War was one of the greatest military tactics in history. The Romans were outsmarted and outmaneuvered, losing tens of thousands of soldiers in a single day.

2. Battle of the Catalaunian Plains (452 AD)

- This battle saw Roman forces, along with their allies, defend against Attila the Hun. Attila had already sacked Rome, but this time, starvation, disease, and a determined Roman defense stopped him. Attila retreated, preserving Rome for a few more years.

3. Siege of Jerusalem (70 AD)

- This was the brutal culmination of the First Jewish–Roman War, where Roman forces, led by Titus, besieged Jerusalem. The Romans built a second wall around the city to cut off all hope for the defenders, eventually leading to the destruction of the Second Temple.

4. Battle of Zela (47 BC)

- Julius Caesar famously dispatched a short message to the Senate after this battle: *"Veni, Vidi, Vici"* ("I came, I saw, I conquered"). Despite being outnumbered, Caesar's forces defeated Pharnaces II of Pontus, demonstrating Roman military superiority.

5. Battle of the Teutoburg Forest (9 AD)

- The Roman army suffered one of its greatest defeats here, losing three entire legions in an ambush led by Arminius, a Germanic leader who had once served Rome. After this defeat, Rome decided the Rhine River would be the empire's northern boundary.

The Building of Hadrian's Wall

Rome's Northernmost Frontier

Hadrian's Wall stands as one of the most enduring symbols of the Roman Empire's reach and determination. Constructed under the orders of Emperor Hadrian in AD 122, this formidable barrier marked the northernmost frontier of the Roman Empire in Britain. Unlike earlier expansionist efforts, Hadrian's approach was one of consolidation and defense, aiming to secure the empire's borders rather than extend them further.

The wall stretched 73 miles across the rugged terrain of northern England, from the River Tyne in the east to the Solway Firth in the west. It wasn't just a simple wall; it was a complex defensive system designed to keep out the fierce Pictish tribes of Scotland and to control the movement of people and goods. The wall was accompanied by a deep ditch, military roads, and a series of fortifications, including milecastles (small fortlets spaced approximately one Roman mile apart) and larger forts housing garrisons.

The construction of Hadrian's Wall was a monumental task, involving thousands of Roman soldiers and local laborers. Built primarily of stone in the eastern sections and turf in the western stretches, the wall was an engineering marvel of its time. Each section was meticulously planned, with forts like Housesteads and Vindolanda serving as hubs of Roman military life on the frontier. These forts were fully equipped with barracks, granaries, and bathhouses, offering a glimpse into the daily lives of the soldiers who manned the wall.

Hadrian's Wall served multiple purposes beyond defense. It was a powerful symbol of Roman authority, a clear demarcation between the civilized world of Rome and the untamed lands of the north. It also functioned as a customs barrier, controlling trade and collecting taxes on goods moving across the frontier.

The wall remained an active military frontier for nearly three centuries, although its significance waned as Rome's influence in Britain declined. Today, Hadrian's Wall is a UNESCO World Heritage Site, attracting visitors from around the world who marvel at this ancient testament to Rome's ambition and engineering prowess.

The Reforms of Diocletian

How Diocletian Divided and Strengthened the Empire

The Roman Empire in the late 3rd century was a colossus teetering on the brink of collapse. Wracked by internal strife, economic turmoil, and external invasions, the empire was in desperate need of reform. Enter Diocletian, a soldier-emperor who rose from humble origins to become one of Rome's most transformative leaders. Upon taking power in AD 284, Diocletian embarked on a series of sweeping reforms that fundamentally changed the structure of the Roman Empire, ensuring its survival for another century and a half. His legacy is one of division, innovation, and relentless focus on stabilizing a crumbling state.

Diocletian's most famous reform was the establishment of the Tetrarchy, a system of rule by four leaders. Recognizing that the vastness of the empire made it impossible for one man to govern effectively, Diocletian divided the empire into two halves: the Eastern and the Western Roman Empires. Each half was ruled by an Augustus (senior emperor) and a Caesar (junior emperor). Diocletian took control of the East, appointing Maximian as Augustus of the West, while Galerius and Constantius Chlorus served as Caesars. This system was designed to provide stability and quick responses to crises across the empire.

By dividing the empire, Diocletian hoped to address the challenges of administering such a vast territory. The Eastern Empire, with its wealthier cities and more defensible borders, was placed under Diocletian's direct control. The Western Empire, which was more exposed to barbarian invasions, was given to Maximian. Each emperor governed his domain semi-independently but under the overarching unity of the Roman state. This division helped to manage the empire's vast resources more effectively and allowed for quicker military and administrative responses to local issues.

Diocletian understood that a strong military was essential for the empire's survival. He reorganized the Roman army, increasing its size and separating it into two main components: the limitanei (border troops) and the comitatenses (mobile field armies). The limitanei were stationed along the frontiers to defend against invasions, while the comitatenses could be rapidly deployed to respond to threats anywhere in the empire. This dual system improved Rome's defensive capabilities and allowed for more flexible military operations.

The Roman economy was in shambles when Diocletian came to power. Rampant inflation, debased currency, and a collapsing tax system threatened the empire's financial stability. To address these issues, Diocletian introduced a series of economic reforms, including a new tax system based on land and population. He also issued the Edict on Maximum Prices in AD 301, which set price controls on goods and wages in an attempt to curb inflation. While this edict was largely unsuccessful and difficult to enforce, it demonstrated Diocletian's commitment to stabilizing the economy.

In addition to his political and economic reforms, Diocletian also sought to strengthen the unity of the empire through religious conformity. He believed that the traditional Roman gods were essential to the empire's success and that the growing Christian population posed a threat to this unity. In AD 303, Diocletian launched what became known as the Diocletianic Persecution, the empire's last and most severe persecution of Christians. Churches were destroyed, scriptures were burned, and many Christians were imprisoned or executed. However, rather than eradicating Christianity, this persecution only strengthened the resolve of the Christian community, setting the stage for the religion's eventual triumph in the Roman world.

To further enhance the efficiency of governance, Diocletian restructured the empire's administrative divisions. He increased the number of provinces from around 50 to over 100, making them smaller and more manageable. These provinces were grouped into larger units called dioceses, each overseen by a vicarius, who reported directly to the emperors. This restructuring reduced the power of provincial governors, curbed corruption, and ensured more direct imperial control over local matters.

Diocletian's reign also saw a significant investment in infrastructure and public works. He commissioned the construction of new roads, bridges, and fortifications across the empire to improve communication and defense. One of his most notable architectural achievements was his own retirement palace in Split (modern-day Croatia), known as Diocletian's Palace. This massive fortress-palace complex was a symbol of his power and remains one of the best-preserved Roman monuments in existence today.

In AD 305, Diocletian did something unprecedented in Roman history: he voluntarily abdicated the throne. Citing health reasons, he retired to his palace in Split, where he spent the remainder of his life tending to his gardens. This act of voluntary retirement was a radical departure from the norm, as Roman emperors typically ruled until they were overthrown or died. Diocletian's abdication set a precedent for future emperors and demonstrated his belief in the importance of orderly succession.

Despite Diocletian's efforts to create a stable system of governance, the Tetrarchy began to unravel after his retirement. Rivalries between the successors led to a series of civil wars, culminating in the rise of Constantine the Great, who ultimately reunited the empire under his sole rule. While the Tetrarchy itself did not last, many of Diocletian's reforms, particularly those related to the military and administration, continued to influence the Roman Empire for years to come.

Diocletian's reforms were crucial in reviving the Roman Empire at a time of near-total collapse. His division of the empire, military restructuring, and administrative innovations provided a framework that helped stabilize the empire and extend its life for another century and a half. While some of his measures, such as the persecution of Christians and the price controls, were less successful, Diocletian's legacy as a reformer and a visionary leader remains undeniable. His reign marked the end of the Crisis of the Third Century and laid the groundwork for the later developments of the Late Roman Empire.

One crazy fact about Diocletian is that after abdicating the throne, he became the only Roman emperor who lived to see his successors in power. Another is that his price control edict, the Edict on Maximum Prices, was one of the earliest attempts at regulating an economy, but it was so widely ignored that it's considered one of the most epic policy failures in history. Diocletian was also the emperor who ordered the last and most brutal persecution of Christians, yet his own palace in Split later became the site of one of the first Christian churches in the region. Lastly, Diocletian's Tetrarchy, while short-lived, inspired later rulers in Europe who admired the idea of shared power as a way to manage vast territories.

Roman Daily Life

Multiple-Choice Quiz on Food, Clothing, and Social Customs

Let's take a stroll through the daily life of ancient Romans! Below are some fun multiple-choice questions that will test your knowledge of Roman food, clothing, and social customs. Imagine yourself in the bustling streets of Rome, surrounded by togas, tasty treats, and intriguing traditions. Ready? Let's dive in!

1. What was the staple food in the diet of most Romans, especially the lower classes?

- a) Rice
- b) Bread
- c) Potatoes
- d) Pasta

2. Which of the following was considered the main meal of the day for Romans, typically eaten in the late afternoon?

- a) Ientaculum (breakfast)
- b) Prandium (lunch)
- c) Cena (dinner)
- d) Merenda (afternoon snack)

3. What type of clothing was most commonly worn by Roman men of all social classes?

- a) Tunica
- b) Toga
- c) Stola
- d) Chiton

4. Which garment was specifically worn by Roman women, especially those of higher status?

   a) Palla
   b) Toga
   c) Tunica
   d) Stola

5. What was the Roman term for the public baths, where Romans would go to bathe, socialize, and relax?

   a) Forum
   b) Insula
   c) Thermae
   d) Domus

6. What sweet treat was a favorite dessert in ancient Rome, often made with honey, nuts, and sometimes cheese?

   a) Pudding
   b) Baklava
   c) Dulcia Domestica
   d) Gelato

7. What did Roman children commonly use as toys in their daily life?

   a) Action figures
   b) Dolls, hoops, and knucklebones
   c) Marbles and dice
   d) Wooden horses and slingshots

8. How did most Romans signal that they were finished with a meal?

   a) By washing their hands in a basin
   b) By clapping their hands
   c) By snapping their fingers
   d) By reclining on their couches

9. What type of footwear was most commonly worn by Romans, both indoors and outdoors?

- a) Boots
- b) Sandals
- c) Loafers
- d) Moccasins

10. In Roman social customs, what was a *patronus*?

- a) A type of weapon
- b) A lawyer in court
- c) A wealthy individual who offered protection and support to clients
- d) A high-ranking soldier

Answers

1. b) Bread

- Bread was the staple food for most Romans, especially for the lower classes. It was often eaten with olive oil, cheese, and sometimes vegetables.

2. c) Cena (dinner)

- Cena was the main meal of the day, usually eaten in the late afternoon or early evening. It was a social event where families and friends gathered to enjoy multiple courses.

3. a) Tunica

- The *tunica* (tunic) was the basic garment worn by Roman men, made of wool or linen, and worn by all social classes. The toga was typically worn over the tunic by men of higher status on formal occasions.

4. d) Stola

- The *stola* was the traditional garment worn by Roman women, especially those of higher status, signifying their marital status.

5. c) Thermae

- The *thermae* were public baths where Romans would go not only to bathe but also to socialize, exercise, and relax. They were an important part of Roman daily life.

6. c) Dulcia Domestica

- *Dulcia Domestica* was a popular Roman dessert made from dates stuffed with nuts, coated in honey, and sometimes mixed with cheese. It was a sweet treat enjoyed at the end of a meal.

7. b) Dolls, hoops, and knucklebones

- Roman children played with a variety of toys, including dolls, hoops, and knucklebones (similar to jacks). These toys were simple but beloved by Roman children.

8. a) By washing their hands in a basin

- After finishing a meal, Romans would often wash their hands in a basin, signaling the end of the dining experience.

9. b) Sandals

- Sandals were the most common type of footwear for Romans, suitable for the warm Mediterranean climate. They were worn by men, women, and children, both indoors and outdoors.

10. c) A wealthy individual who offered protection and support to clients

- A *patronus* was a wealthy Roman who offered protection, financial support, and legal assistance to clients in exchange for loyalty and services. This relationship was a key aspect of Roman social structure.

Roman Jokes

A Glimpse into Ancient Humor

Romans were known for their grand architecture, military prowess, and philosophical musings, but did you know they also had a sense of humor? Even in ancient Rome, people enjoyed a good laugh, often poking fun at everyday life, social norms, and even the gods. While some of these jokes might seem a bit old-fashioned today, they give us a unique insight into the lighter side of Roman culture. Let's explore some of the jokes that might have tickled the funny bones of ancient Romans—and who knows, you might find yourself chuckling too!

1. The Absent-Minded Professor

"A philosopher is asked, 'What's the difference between a philosopher and a pigeon?' The philosopher thinks for a moment and replies, 'I give up, what?' The questioner responds, 'The pigeon can reach a conclusion!'"

- Even back in ancient Rome, philosophers had a reputation for overthinking things. This joke playfully mocks their tendency to get lost in their thoughts and never really come to a decisive answer—something we can all relate to when we're caught in a mental loop!

2. The Lazy Barber

"A man with a long beard walks into a barber shop. The barber asks, 'Would you like me to trim your beard or shave it off?' The man replies, 'Neither, I just came to remind you that you're still in business.'"

- This joke pokes fun at the sometimes-lackadaisical attitude of barbers (and perhaps service providers in general). The man with the long beard clearly hasn't needed a trim in ages, but he drops by just to remind the barber that he still exists—showing that even in Rome, people had to deal with slow service!

3. The Patient Doctor

"A patient says to his doctor, 'It hurts when I do this,' raising his arm. The doctor replies, 'Then don't do that!'"

- This classic joke has ancient roots! The Romans loved humor that revolved around practical wisdom (or lack thereof). The doctor's advice is simple, direct, and humorously unhelpful, playing on the idea that sometimes the most obvious solution is the one right in front of us.

4. The Miser's Will

"A miser on his deathbed tells his son, 'Promise me that when I die, you'll place all my money in my coffin.' The son agrees, but after the miser's death, he deposits a small bag of coins in the coffin. 'What about the rest?' someone asks. The son replies, 'I wrote him a check for the balance!'"

- Even in ancient Rome, misers were fair game for jokes. This one is a playful jab at the stingy, highlighting the absurdity of taking wealth to the grave. The son's clever solution—writing a check instead of burying real money—adds a timeless twist to the humor.

5. The Absent Friend

"A Roman senator is asked why he wasn't at a friend's funeral. He replies, 'The funeral is for the dead, not for the living. If you die, I'll be there!'"

- This joke plays on the idea of prioritizing the living over the dead, with a senator making a tongue-in-cheek excuse for skipping a friend's funeral. It's a reminder that, even in Rome, people could be just as cheeky when it came to their social obligations.

6. The Student and the Teacher

"A teacher asks his student, 'What do we call a man who avoids hard work?' The student quickly answers, 'A genius!'"

- This one shows that students haven't changed much in the last 2,000 years. The quick-witted reply from the student turns what could have been a lesson on laziness into a joke about cleverness—after all, who wouldn't want to be called a genius?

7. The Gods Are Watching

"Jupiter asks Mercury, 'Why do people on Earth always ask me for wealth and success, but never for wisdom?' Mercury replies, 'Because they want to look smart, not be smart.'"

- Romans often made light of their gods, humanizing them in jokes. This one highlights the vanity of people who seek wealth and success over wisdom, with the gods themselves acknowledging human nature's little quirks.

Roman humor may have been different from what we're used to today, but it's clear that they enjoyed a good laugh just like we do. These jokes give us a glimpse into the everyday lives of Romans, revealing their playful side and reminding us that humor is a universal human experience—even across the millennia.

Roman Law and Governance Influences the World Today

The influence of Roman law on modern legal systems is profound and far-reaching. Many of the principles and structures that underpin contemporary legal frameworks can trace their origins back to ancient Rome. Here's a look at how Roman law has shaped modern-day legal systems:

1. The Concept of Written Law: The Twelve Tables

The idea that laws should be written down and publicly accessible is one of the most significant legacies of Roman law. The Twelve Tables, created around 450 BC, were the first attempt by the Romans to establish a codified legal system. These laws covered various aspects of daily life, from property rights to family law, and were displayed in public so that all citizens could know their rights and obligations. This concept of codified, publicly accessible laws is a cornerstone of modern legal systems.

2. The Principle of Legal Precedent

Roman law introduced the concept of *stare decisis*, or legal precedent, which means that past judicial decisions should be followed in future cases with similar circumstances. This principle ensures consistency and fairness in the application of the law, and it remains a fundamental aspect of common law systems today, particularly in countries like the United States and the United Kingdom.

3. Civil Law Systems

The Roman legal system heavily influenced the development of civil law, which is the foundation of legal systems in many European and

Latin American countries. The *Corpus Juris Civilis* (Body of Civil Law), compiled under the Byzantine Emperor Justinian in the 6th century AD, codified Roman law and became a reference point for later legal systems in Europe. Modern civil law codes, such as the French *Code Napoléon* and the German *Bürgerliches Gesetzbuch (BGB)*, are directly descended from Roman law.

4. Property Rights

Roman law laid the groundwork for modern property rights, including concepts like ownership, possession, and transfer of property. The distinctions made by Roman jurists between different types of property and ownership have been adopted and adapted by contemporary legal systems. For example, the idea of private property, where individuals have the exclusive right to use and dispose of their possessions, is rooted in Roman legal thought.

5. Contracts and Obligations

The Roman law of contracts and obligations has had a lasting impact on modern contract law. Roman jurists developed detailed rules about how contracts should be formed, what obligations they created, and how they could be enforced. These principles are still evident in today's legal frameworks, where contracts are fundamental to business transactions, employment agreements, and more.

6. Criminal Law

Roman law introduced several concepts that continue to shape modern criminal law. For instance, the notion that the accused is presumed innocent until proven guilty has its origins in Roman legal practices. Additionally, the Romans developed detailed procedures for trials, including the rights of the accused to a fair hearing and the importance of evidence, which have carried over into contemporary judicial processes.

7. Legal Terminology

Many legal terms used today are derived directly from Latin, the language of Roman law. Words like *"jury," "justice," "verdict,"* and *"subpoena"* all have their roots in Roman legal language. This continuity of terminology reflects the enduring influence of Roman law on modern legal discourse.

8. The Role of Legal Professionals

Roman law also established the roles of legal professionals such as advocates (similar to modern-day lawyers) and judges. The Roman emphasis on specialized legal knowledge and the importance of legal experts in interpreting and applying the law is a tradition that has continued into the modern era. Today, the training and role of lawyers, judges, and legal scholars are deeply rooted in the Roman legal tradition.

9. Equality Before the Law

One of the key principles of Roman law was that all citizens should be equal before the law, regardless of their social status. This idea, though not always perfectly implemented in ancient Rome, laid the foundation for the modern concept of legal equality. In contemporary legal systems, the notion that everyone is subject to the law and has the right to equal protection under the law is a core principle.

10. Influence on International Law

Roman law's influence extends beyond national borders to the realm of international law. The Roman concepts of *jus gentium* (law of nations) and *jus naturale* (natural law) have informed the development of international legal principles, particularly in areas like human rights and diplomatic relations. The idea that certain laws and rights are universal and should be respected across different cultures and societies owes much to Roman legal philosophy.

In summary, the legal systems of today are deeply indebted to the innovations and principles developed in ancient Rome. Whether it's the structure of legal codes, the procedures of courts, or the language of the law, the legacy of Roman law continues to be felt in every aspect of modern jurisprudence. The Romans not only provided the foundations for many legal systems but also laid down ideas of justice, rights, and equality that remain central to our understanding of the law today.

Roman Entertainment

True or False Quiz

Let's dive into the world of Roman entertainment! From gladiatorial games to chariot races, the Romans knew how to keep their citizens entertained. But how much do you really know about their favorite pastimes?

1. **True or False:** Gladiatorial games were originally held as part of funeral rites to honor the deceased.
2. **True or False:** The Colosseum could be flooded to host naval battles, known as *naumachiae*.
3. **True or False:** Chariot racing was one of the least popular forms of entertainment in ancient Rome.
4. **True or False:** Roman theaters often featured comedies and tragedies similar to those of ancient Greece, but with more slapstick humor and improvisation.
5. **True or False:** The Romans invented the concept of the "stadium wave" during their chariot races.
6. **True or False:** Animals from all over the Roman Empire, including lions, elephants, and crocodiles, were used in the Colosseum for various spectacles.
7. **True or False:** Roman banquets often included live musical performances, poetry readings, and even staged mock debates for entertainment.
8. **True or False:** Women were not allowed to attend public games and spectacles in the Colosseum.
9. **True or False:** Public executions were sometimes carried out as part of the entertainment during Roman games.

10. **True or False:** The Circus Maximus, where chariot races were held, could seat up to 250,000 spectators, making it the largest stadium in ancient Rome.

Answers

1. True

- Gladiatorial games did indeed originate as part of funeral rites, where the bloodshed was believed to appease the spirits of the dead. Over time, these games became public spectacles detached from funerary contexts.

2. True

- The Colosseum could be flooded to stage mock naval battles called *naumachiae*. These events were grand spectacles that demonstrated Roman engineering prowess and entertained thousands of spectators.

3. False

- Chariot racing was actually one of the most popular forms of entertainment in ancient Rome. The races, held in the Circus Maximus, attracted huge crowds and fierce fan loyalty, much like modern-day sports.

4. True

- Roman theater was heavily influenced by Greek drama but incorporated more slapstick humor, farce, and improvisation. Romans loved a good laugh, and their comedies often poked fun at everyday life.

5. False

- The "stadium wave" is a modern phenomenon and wasn't part of ancient Roman chariot races. However, the Romans did have their own ways of showing enthusiasm, such as shouting, cheering, and waving garments.

6. True

- Romans imported exotic animals from across the empire for use in the Colosseum. These animals were often pitted against each other, against gladiators, or used in hunting displays for the entertainment of the masses.

7. True

- Roman banquets were not just about food and drink; they were social occasions that included various forms of entertainment, such as music, poetry readings, and intellectual debates to amuse and impress guests.

8. False

- Women were allowed to attend public games and spectacles in the Colosseum, though seating was segregated, with women generally sitting in the upper tiers.

9. True

- Public executions were indeed a part of Roman entertainment, often conducted in the Colosseum during games. These grim spectacles were intended to demonstrate the power of the state and deter criminal behavior.

10. True

- The Circus Maximus was the largest stadium in ancient Rome, capable of seating up to 250,000 spectators. It was the epicenter of chariot racing, a sport that captivated Roman audiences for centuries.

Roman Literature

Match the Author to Their Famous Work

Let's dive into the rich world of Roman literature! Below are multiple-choice questions where you'll match famous Roman authors to their most iconic works. Afterward, you'll find the answers along with fascinating details about each author and their contributions. Ready to test your knowledge?

1. Virgil - Which epic poem did Virgil, one of Rome's greatest poets, write? This work tells the story of Aeneas, a Trojan hero whose journey leads to the founding of Rome.

- a) Metamorphoses
- b) The Aeneid
- c) Satires

2. Cicero -Cicero, a statesman, orator, and philosopher, is known for his speeches and writings that defended the Roman Republic's principles. Which of his works is a philosophical treatise on the nature of the gods and human happiness?

- a) De Rerum Natura
- b) De Officiis
- c) De Natura Deorum

3. Ovid -Ovid was a master of elegiac couplets and one of Rome's most beloved poets. Which of his works is a collection of mythological tales that explore themes of transformation and love?

- a) The Aeneid
- b) Metamorphoses
- c) Histories

4. Seneca - Seneca was a Stoic philosopher, playwright, and advisor to Emperor Nero. Which work is a collection of essays and letters that offer practical advice on how to live a virtuous and serene life?

- a) Meditations
- b) Letters to Lucilius
- c) De Bello Gallico

5. Horace - Horace, another major Roman poet, is famous for his *Odes*, but which work is a collection of poems that provide witty observations on the art of living and satire?

- a) Satires
- b) Epodes
- c) De Architectura

6. Livy - Livy was a Roman historian whose monumental history of Rome spans the city's legendary founding through its rise to dominance. What is the title of this vast historical work?

- a) Annals
- b) Ab Urbe Condita
- c) Histories

7. Juvenal - Juvenal is known for his biting satirical poems that critiqued the moral decay and social issues of Roman society. Which work is his most famous collection of satirical poems?

- a) Satires
- b) Georgics
- c) Epistulae

8. Tacitus Tacitus was one of Rome's greatest historians, known for his concise and insightful analysis of the Roman Empire. Which of his works details the history of Rome from the reign of Tiberius to Nero?

- a) Germania
- b) Annals
- c) Ab Urbe Condita

9. Plautus - Plautus was one of the earliest Roman playwrights, famous for his comedic plays that were full of witty dialogue and humorous plots. Which work is one of his most famous comedies?

- a) Pseudolus
- b) Medea
- c) Pharsalia

10. Lucretius - Lucretius was a poet and philosopher who wrote a didactic poem that explores Epicurean philosophy and the nature of the universe. What is the title of this work?

- a) De Rerum Natura
- b) Georgics
- c) Annals

Answers and Explanations

1. b) The Aeneid

- *The Aeneid* is Virgil's masterpiece, an epic poem that traces the journey of Aeneas, a Trojan hero, from the ruins of Troy to the shores of Italy, where he lays the foundation for the future city of Rome. Commissioned by Emperor Augustus, *The Aeneid* was intended to glorify Rome's origins and Augustus's reign by connecting them to the heroic past. Virgil's rich, poetic language and complex characters have made this work a cornerstone of Western literature, influencing countless authors and artists throughout history.

2. c) De Natura Deorum

- Cicero's *De Natura Deorum* (On the Nature of the Gods) is a philosophical dialogue that delves into Roman religious beliefs, comparing the theological views of the Epicureans, Stoics, and Academics. Written in 45 BC, this work showcases Cicero's mastery of rhetoric and philosophy. It is particularly notable for its examination of the gods' nature and their role in human affairs, making it an essential text for understanding Roman thought and its influence on later Western philosophy, particularly during the Renaissance.

3. b) Metamorphoses

- Ovid's *Metamorphoses* is a sprawling epic composed of over 250 myths, all connected by the theme of transformation. From gods turning mortals into animals or plants to humans transforming into constellations, Ovid's imaginative and often playful retelling of these myths has captivated readers for centuries. Written in a flowing, continuous narrative, *Metamorphoses* is not only a rich source of mythology but also a profound exploration of change as a fundamental aspect of existence. This work has inspired countless works of art, literature, and even psychology.

4. b) Letters to Lucilius

- Seneca's *Letters to Lucilius* is a collection of moral epistles that offer practical advice on living a good and virtuous life according to Stoic principles. Written in the form of letters to his friend Lucilius, these essays cover a wide range of topics, from dealing with adversity to the nature of friendship. Seneca's writing is both deeply philosophical and intensely personal, reflecting his own struggles and insights as a statesman and philosopher. His *Letters* have had a lasting impact on Stoic thought and continue to be a source of inspiration for those seeking wisdom and tranquility in a turbulent world.

5. a) Satires

- Horace's *Satires* are a witty and insightful collection of poems that explore the social mores and everyday life of Rome. With his trademark humor and light touch, Horace critiques the vices and follies of his contemporaries, offering wisdom on how to live a balanced and fulfilling life. Unlike the harsher satires of Juvenal, Horace's approach is more genial, often poking fun at himself as well. His work has influenced a long line of satirists, from Alexander Pope to Mark Twain, and remains a delightful read for those interested in the art of living well.

6. b) Ab Urbe Condita

- Livy's *Ab Urbe Condita* (From the Founding of the City) is a monumental history of Rome, covering its mythical origins through to the Augustan era. Though much of this vast work has been lost, the surviving books provide a detailed account of Rome's early history, including its legendary kings and the Republic's battles against foreign enemies. Livy's narrative is not just a chronicle of events; it is a moral history, celebrating the virtues that made Rome great and warning against the vices that could lead to its downfall. His work has shaped the way Romans and later generations understood their past and the values they held dear.

7. a) Satires

- Juvenal's *Satires* are some of the most powerful critiques of Roman society ever written. Known for their biting wit and moral indignation, these poems expose the corruption, decadence, and hypocrisy of Rome's elite. Juvenal's satirical style is direct and uncompromising, making his work a timeless commentary on power and morality. His influence extends far beyond his own time, inspiring satirists like Jonathan Swift and George Orwell, who also used humor to critique social and political issues.

8. b) Annals

- Tacitus's *Annals* is a detailed history of the Roman Empire, covering the reigns of Tiberius, Caligula, Claudius, and Nero. Written with a sharp, concise style, Tacitus offers a penetrating analysis of the corruption and tyranny that plagued the Roman state during this period. His work is not just a record of events but a commentary on the moral and political decay of Rome's ruling class. Tacitus's insights into power and human nature have made *Annals* a classic of historical writing, influencing both historians and political theorists.

9. a) Pseudolus

- Plautus's *Pseudolus* is one of his most famous comedies, filled with clever dialogue, humorous misunderstandings, and engaging characters. Written in the early 2nd century BC, this play showcases Plautus's talent for adapting Greek comedic tropes to a Roman audience. *Pseudolus* tells the story of a clever slave who outwits his master and others to secure the freedom of a young woman in love. The play is a brilliant example of Roman comedy's emphasis on wit, social satire, and the triumph of the underdog, and it remains influential in the history of Western theater.

10. a) De Rerum Natura

- Lucretius's *De Rerum Natura* (On the Nature of Things) is a didactic poem that explores Epicurean philosophy, particularly the nature of the universe, the soul, and the gods. Written in the 1st century BC, this work seeks to free its readers from the fear of death and the unknown by explaining the world in purely natural terms. Lucretius's poetic treatment of complex philosophical ideas has made *De Rerum Natura* a masterpiece of both literature and philosophy, influencing thinkers from the Renaissance to the Enlightenment who sought to reconcile science and humanism.

Why Do Men Think About the Roman Empire So Much?

TikTok Wants to Know

There's a new trend on TikTok that's got everyone asking: *Why are men so obsessed with the Roman Empire?* It all started when women began casually asking the men in their lives a seemingly simple question: "How often do you think about the Roman Empire?" The answers, often delivered with the utmost seriousness, were surprising, to say the least. Turns out, many men think about the Roman Empire—a lot. Like, more than once a week. Sometimes even daily. And the responses have women across TikTok scratching their heads in bewilderment, while the men just keep on mentally marching through ancient Rome.

So, what's going on here? Why are men so fascinated by a civilization that peaked over 1,500 years ago? The trend taps into a classic "men are from Mars, women are from Venus" scenario that has been fodder for comedians for years. Women are amused and confused, while men casually discuss the strategic genius of Julius Caesar, the engineering marvels of Roman aqueducts, or the epic battles that shaped the world. It's a peek into the inner workings of the male brain, where thoughts of ancient history apparently lurk just beneath the surface, waiting to bubble up at the slightest prompt.

The origins of this viral phenomenon can be traced back to Instagram, where Swedish influencer Saskia Cort first planted the idea in 2022, telling her followers to ask their male partners how often they think about the Roman Empire. Fast forward to August 2023, and the trend made a comeback, thanks to history enthusiast Gaius Flavius, who reignited the question with an Instagram reel that sent the meme spiraling into TikTok's mainstream consciousness.

But why the Roman Empire specifically? There's something undeniably compelling about the grandeur and drama of Rome's history. It's got everything: epic battles, political intrigue, monumental architecture, and a legendary fall from grace. Ridley Scott's *Gladiator* and HBO's *Rome* likely played a part in popularizing this era, making it feel almost like a part of our collective cultural memory. And let's not forget the aesthetic—those helmets, the togas, the grand coliseums. There's just something about the Roman Empire that keeps it lodged in the minds of men everywhere, like an ancient pop culture reference that never fades away.

Perhaps it's the contrast between the warrior spirit of ancient Rome and the often more sedentary modern life that draws men in. The Roman Empire represents a time when life was lived on the edge, where every decision could mean the difference between glory and disaster. It's a far cry from the daily grind of office work, and maybe that's the appeal—a mental escape to a time of sword fights and conquests, where men were men, and empires rose and fell on the strength of their will.

Of course, the Roman Empire isn't the only historical obsession men tend to have. The American Civil War, WWII, and the lives of historical figures like Napoleon and Alexander the Great also have their own devoted fan clubs. But there's something about Rome—its sheer scale, the dramatic rise and fall, the mix of brutality and sophistication—that makes it a particularly enduring fixation.

In the end, the Roman Empire's grip on the male imagination is just another example of how history, with all its drama and grandeur, continues to resonate in unexpected ways. And thanks to TikTok, we now know that while women might be pondering their next shopping trip or the latest Netflix series, the men in their lives are silently strategizing like Caesar or constructing aqueducts in their minds.

So next time you catch your partner staring off into the distance, don't be surprised if they're not thinking about work or dinner plans—but about how they would have improved the defenses of Rome. And as TikTok has shown us, this quirky historical obsession is one shared by men across the globe, uniting them in a brotherhood of ancient history nerds, one Roman Empire at a time.

The Sack of Rome by the Visigoths

The Fall of an Eternal Empire

For centuries, Rome was a city that seemed untouchable. It wasn't just the capital of an empire; it was the beating heart of Western civilization, with roads that stretched across continents, legions that commanded fear, and a culture that thrived in the arts, architecture, and law. But even the greatest empires have a breaking point, and in 410 AD, the unimaginable happened: Rome, after standing tall for 800 years, fell to a foreign enemy.

That enemy? The Visigoths, led by their determined and frustrated king, Alaric. For years, the Visigoths had been playing a long game of political tug-of-war with the Roman Empire. These so-called "barbarians" (a term that the Romans slapped on anyone who wasn't, well, Roman) had been bouncing around the empire, trying to find a place to settle. But Rome, in its typical imperial arrogance, kept them on the edge, promising and withdrawing, all while watching the Visigoths' patience run thin.

By 410 AD, Alaric had had enough. The Visigoths, who had once fought alongside the Romans as allies, were now positioned as their greatest threat. Alaric marched his people right to the gates of Rome, and to the shock of the world, the eternal city's defenses crumbled.

Rome had been sacked. The first time in 800 years that the mighty city had been overrun by a foreign army. It wasn't just any army; it was the Visigoths, a group that the Romans had always seen as outsiders, the "uncivilized" people from the wilderness beyond the empire's borders. But here they were, inside the very heart of Rome, looting and pillaging to their hearts' content.

The city was a shadow of its former self, both politically and economically weakened by years of internal decay. Gone were the days of Julius Caesar's triumphs and Augustus's golden era. Now, it was a Rome that had seen better days, stuck in a desperate struggle to hold onto its past glories.

But let's be clear: while the sack was a massive blow to Roman prestige, it wasn't the complete and utter destruction of the city. In fact, Alaric and his Visigoths were relatively "civilized" about the whole thing. They didn't slaughter the populace wholesale or burn the city to the ground. It was more of a strategic plunder—a grab at wealth, resources, and influence. Still, it sent a clear message: Rome was no longer invincible.

So, how did it come to this? How did Rome, the once-unassailable fortress of civilization, fall to a wandering group of Visigoths?

Well, the answer lies in a mix of bad decisions, political infighting, and overextended borders. By the time of the sack, Rome wasn't the empire it once was. It had split into East and West, with the Western half (the part Alaric and his crew invaded) suffering from weak leadership, constant civil wars, and dwindling resources. The Roman military, once the pride of the world, was now a skeleton force, scattered and undermanned.

For the Visigoths, this was an opportunity they couldn't pass up. Alaric wasn't just looking for spoils; he was looking for a home for his people. The sack was as much a political statement as it was a raid.

Interestingly, while the fall of Rome to the Visigoths was a significant marker in history, it wasn't the end of the Roman Empire—not just yet, anyway. The empire limped along for a few more decades, with its final collapse coming in 476 AD when the last Roman emperor in the West, Romulus Augustulus, was deposed.

The sack of Rome, however, symbolized the beginning of the end. It was the first loud crack in the empire's seemingly impenetrable armor. To the Romans, the event was earth-shattering. To the rest of the world, it was a reminder that even the mightiest fall—and when they do, they fall hard.

As for the Visigoths, they didn't stay in Rome for long. After collecting their loot, they moved on, eventually settling in what we now call Spain and parts of Southern France, leaving Rome in its bruised, battered state to reflect on its former glory.

Did You Know?

- Despite the terror and destruction, some Romans believed that the sack of Rome was a divine punishment for abandoning the old pagan gods in favor of Christianity. Talk about holding a grudge!
- Alaric didn't actually want to destroy Rome; he saw himself as more of a "liberator" who just wanted what was owed to his people. He even allowed certain sacred sites to remain untouched. Not your average barbarian.
- The fall of Rome wasn't the last time the city was sacked. It would happen again in 455 AD, this time by the Vandals. Seems like Rome just couldn't catch a break.

The Sack of Rome by the Visigoths wasn't just a singular event—it was a seismic shift in the history of Western civilization. It marked the decline of the Roman Empire and the rise of the so-called "barbarian kingdoms" that would dominate Europe for centuries to come. For the Romans, it was a moment of reckoning, and for the rest of the world, it was a reminder that no empire, no matter how powerful, is invincible.

Julius Caesar's Life and Legacy Quiz

Questions:

1. What year was Julius Caesar born?

    a) 100 BC
    b) 44 BC
    c) 50 BC
    d) 63 BC

2. Caesar formed a political alliance known as the First Triumvirate. Who were the other two members?

    a) Pompey and Crassus
    b) Mark Antony and Octavian
    c) Sulla and Cicero
    d) Brutus and Cassius

3. Which of Caesar's military campaigns made him famous and expanded Rome's territory into what is now France?

    a) The Gallic Wars
    b) The Punic Wars
    c) The Macedonian Wars
    d) The Samnite Wars

4. What significant event occurred when Julius Caesar crossed the Rubicon River in 49 BC?

    a) He declared himself dictator for life
    b) He began a civil war against Pompey and the Roman Senate
    c) He became the emperor of Rome
    d) He conquered Egypt

5. Who was Caesar's famous lover and political ally in Egypt?

   a) Cleopatra
   b) Nefertiti
   c) Hatshepsut
   d) Berenice

6. What title did Julius Caesar hold at the time of his assassination?

   a) Emperor
   b) King
   c) Dictator for life
   d) Consul

7. On what date was Julius Caesar assassinated?

   a) March 15, 44 BC
   b) April 1, 45 BC
   c) January 10, 50 BC
   d) May 5, 46 BC

8. Which two senators were key leaders in the plot to assassinate Julius Caesar?

   a) Brutus and Cassius
   b) Pompey and Cicero
   c) Octavian and Lepidus
   d) Sulla and Cato

9. What famous phrase is attributed to Julius Caesar as he was assassinated?

   a) "I came, I saw, I conquered"
   b) "Beware the Ides of March"
   c) "Et tu, Brute?"
   d) "The die is cast"

10. What was the long-term effect of Caesar's assassination on the Roman Republic?

    a) Rome immediately returned to a democracy

b) Rome was plunged into another civil war
c) Caesar's death brought peace to Rome
d) Rome became part of the Egyptian Empire

Answers

1. What year was Julius Caesar born?

Answer: A) 100 BC

- Julius Caesar was born on July 12, 100 BC, into the powerful Julian family. His birth came during the waning years of the Roman Republic, setting the stage for his rise to power during a time of political upheaval.

2. Caesar formed a political alliance known as the First Triumvirate. Who were the other two members?

Answer: A) Pompey and Crassus

- The First Triumvirate was an informal political alliance between Julius Caesar, Pompey the Great, and Marcus Licinius Crassus. They combined their resources to dominate Roman politics, though this alliance would later unravel, leading to a civil war between Caesar and Pompey.

3. Which of Caesar's military campaigns made him famous and expanded Rome's territory into what is now France?

Answer: A) The Gallic Wars

- The Gallic Wars, waged from 58 BC to 50 BC, were a series of military campaigns led by Julius Caesar that resulted in the Roman conquest of Gaul (modern-day France). This victory solidified Caesar's reputation as a brilliant military commander and expanded Roman influence.

4. What significant event occurred when Julius Caesar crossed the Rubicon River in 49 BC?

Answer: B) He began a civil war against Pompey and the Roman Senate

- Caesar's crossing of the Rubicon River with his army in 49 BC was a direct act of defiance against the Roman Senate, effectively starting a civil war. The phrase "crossing the Rubicon" is now synonymous with passing the point of no return.

5. Who was Caesar's famous lover and political ally in Egypt?

Answer: A) Cleopatra

- Caesar had a romantic and political alliance with Cleopatra, the Queen of Egypt. Their relationship was strategic, as Cleopatra sought Roman support in her rule, while Caesar was captivated by her intelligence and charm.

6. What title did Julius Caesar hold at the time of his assassination?

Answer: C) Dictator for life

- Julius Caesar was declared "dictator for life" in 44 BC, giving him almost absolute power. His growing authority and bypassing of traditional Republican governance led to concerns that he aimed to become a monarch, prompting his assassination.

7. On what date was Julius Caesar assassinated?

Answer: A) March 15, 44 BC

- Julius Caesar was assassinated on the Ides of March (March 15) in 44 BC, a date that became famous due to the ominous warning given to him to "beware the Ides of March." His assassination took place in the Senate, where he was stabbed 23 times by his rivals.

8. Which two senators were key leaders in the plot to assassinate Julius Caesar?

Answer: A) Brutus and Cassius

- Marcus Junius Brutus and Gaius Cassius Longinus were the leading figures behind Caesar's assassination. Brutus was particularly significant because he had once been a close ally of Caesar, which made his betrayal a dramatic and symbolic act.

9. What famous phrase is attributed to Julius Caesar as he was assassinated?

Answer: C) "Et tu, Brute?"

- According to Shakespeare's play *Julius Caesar*, the dictator's last words were "Et tu, Brute?" (meaning "And you, Brutus?"), spoken in disbelief as his close friend Brutus joined the assassination. Historically, this phrase's accuracy is debated, but it's become part of Caesar's legacy.

10. What was the long-term effect of Caesar's assassination on the Roman Republic?

Answer: B) Rome was plunged into another civil war

- Far from saving the Republic, Caesar's assassination led to a series of civil wars as his supporters and rivals vied for power. Eventually, Caesar's adopted heir, Octavian (later Augustus), emerged victorious, marking the end of the Roman Republic and the beginning of the Roman Empire.

The Life of Marcus Aurelius

The Philosopher-Emperor and His Contributions to Rome

Marcus Aurelius, often called the philosopher-emperor, is one of those rare historical figures who ruled an empire and still found time to pen one of the greatest philosophical works of all time. Imagine running Rome by day and contemplating the meaning of life by night. That's Marcus for you—a multitasker in the truest sense.

Born in 121 AD, Marcus didn't exactly grow up expecting to be the emperor. But fate (and some well-placed family connections) nudged him into the seat of power. His reign from 161 to 180 AD is remembered as the last of the *Pax Romana*, a golden age of relative peace and prosperity. But unlike most emperors, Marcus wasn't all about conquest and glory. No, this guy had a different kind of ambition: wisdom.

Marcus Aurelius is best known today for his work *Meditations*, a series of personal writings on Stoic philosophy. Imagine being so deep in your thoughts that you start jotting down wisdom like, "The happiness of your life depends upon the quality of your thoughts." For Marcus, ruling an empire was important, but mastering the self was crucial. *Meditations* wasn't meant for public consumption (who knew that centuries later people would be buying this stuff off the shelves?), but it gives us a window into the mind of a man who grappled with power, responsibility, and human frailty.

But don't let the philosopher vibe fool you—Marcus had his share of real-world challenges too. His reign was plagued by wars on the frontiers, particularly against Germanic tribes. While Marcus would have probably preferred to spend his time pondering the nature of virtue, he had to suit up for battle more often than not. Yet even amid war, he maintained his Stoic calm, famously writing, "The art of living is more like wrestling than dancing."

Beyond philosophy and war, Marcus Aurelius also worked hard to stabilize the Roman economy, enacted laws to help the poor, and upheld Roman traditions. He truly embodied that tricky balance between philosopher and ruler, managing to reflect on the universe while handling the nitty-gritty of running the world's most powerful empire.

But every silver lining has a cloud, and for Marcus, that cloud came in the form of his son, Commodus. The guy was... let's just say, *not* the philosopher-emperor type. After Marcus's death, Commodus took the throne, and things went downhill pretty fast. But that's another story.

In the end, Marcus Aurelius left behind more than a legacy of leadership. He left behind words that still resonate, a reminder that wisdom, humility, and strength are the true marks of a great ruler—even when you're dealing with barbarians at the gate.

The Mystery of the Lost Legion

The Disappearance of the Ninth Legion in Britain

Ah, the Ninth Legion—a Roman military unit so legendary that even their *disappearance* became stuff of myth. Picture this: a legion of hardened Roman soldiers marching into the wilds of Britain, never to be seen again. Sounds like the plot of a Netflix special, doesn't it?

The Ninth Legion, also known as *Legio IX Hispana*, had quite the resume. They were battle-hardened, having fought in Spain, the Gallic Wars, and even quashed rebellions in Britain. But somewhere between their postings in the northern reaches of Britain—land of mist, moors, and the occasionally peeved Pictish warrior—the Ninth simply vanished from the historical record around 120 AD. That's where the mystery begins.

So, what happened? Historians have been debating this for centuries. One theory is that the Ninth was utterly destroyed in battle, possibly during a revolt by native British tribes. If you've ever seen the rugged landscapes of Scotland, you'll know it's the kind of place where an entire Roman legion could easily be ambushed and overwhelmed by fierce warriors using the terrain to their advantage. The Romans may have been good at building roads, but the Picts were excellent at guerrilla warfare.

Another idea suggests that the Ninth wasn't wiped out in Britain at all but was instead relocated elsewhere in the empire. Maybe they were sent to the eastern provinces to fight Parthians, or perhaps they were quietly disbanded due to heavy losses. Either way, the Ninth simply fades from Roman records, leaving a giant question mark over their fate.

But let's be honest: the idea that an entire legion was erased in the mists of Britain is too tantalizing to resist. It's the stuff of legends. Stories about the Ninth's disappearance have inspired countless novels, films, and wild theories. Some have even speculated that they met a mystical end, falling victim to curses or supernatural forces in the mysterious north. Of course, that's a bit of a stretch—but hey, history is way more fun when you sprinkle in a little magic, right?

The real answer may forever remain a mystery, but one thing's for sure: the story of the Ninth Legion captures the imagination. Whether they were wiped out by a fierce tribe, reassigned, or simply lost in bureaucratic shuffle, the idea of Roman soldiers marching off into the unknown—never to return—keeps us wondering what *really* happened in the foggy frontiers of ancient Britain.

The Dacian Wars

Trajan's Campaigns and the Story Behind the Trajan Column

When Emperor Trajan set his sights on Dacia (modern-day Romania), he wasn't just looking for a quick win—he was aiming to make history. And, boy, did he succeed. Trajan's Dacian Wars, fought between 101 and 106 AD, not only expanded the Roman Empire but also left us with one of the most famous monuments in ancient history: the Trajan Column.

First, a little backstory. Dacia, under the rule of King Decebalus, had been a constant thorn in Rome's side for years. Decebalus was crafty, skilled in guerrilla tactics, and had a knack for causing trouble on Rome's northeastern frontier. Trajan, however, wasn't one to shy away from a challenge. He launched two campaigns against Dacia, determined to bring the kingdom into the fold of the Roman Empire.

The first war (101-102 AD) was a series of fierce battles. Trajan managed to defeat Decebalus, but instead of destroying him, he offered the Dacian king relatively lenient terms, allowing him to keep his throne. Big mistake. Decebalus quickly broke the peace and started causing trouble again. So, in 105 AD, Trajan returned for round two—this time with no mercy.

The second campaign was brutal. Trajan's legions stormed into Dacia, laying siege to its strongholds and cutting off Decebalus's escape routes. Eventually, the Dacian king, rather than be captured, took his own life. With Dacia finally subdued, Rome annexed the territory, gaining control of its rich gold mines—making the conquest not just a strategic win, but an economic one too.

And how did Trajan celebrate? By erecting a *giant* column, of course! The Trajan Column, still standing in Rome today, is an epic stone comic strip that spirals upward, depicting the key moments of the Dacian Wars. From Trajan addressing his troops to the Romans constructing bridges and fortresses, every aspect of the campaign is immortalized in intricate carvings. Think of it as ancient propaganda—but with a lot more flair.

The column is about 100 feet tall and serves as a testament to Roman engineering. Not only does it tell the story of Trajan's victories, but it also showcases the might and sophistication of the Roman Empire. It's an incredible piece of art and history all rolled into one—and a reminder that when Trajan went to war, he didn't just fight for territory. He fought for a legacy.

In the end, Trajan's Dacian campaigns cemented his reputation as one of Rome's greatest emperors. And while Dacia may have been absorbed into the empire, Trajan's column stands tall—literally—as a monument to Roman ambition, artistry, and the emperor's enduring desire to be remembered as a conqueror.

Roman Roads and Aqueducts

True or False Quiz

1. **True or False?** Roman roads were originally built just for military purposes.
2. **True or False?** The famous saying "All roads lead to Rome" reflects the vast network of Roman roads that connected the empire.
3. **True or False?** Roman roads were typically made of cobblestones, sand, and clay, and were not very durable.
4. **True or False?** Aqueducts were solely built to carry drinking water to Roman cities.
5. **True or False?** The Pont du Gard in France is one of the most famous examples of a Roman aqueduct still standing today.
6. **True or False?** Roman engineers developed a system to purify the water carried by aqueducts before it reached the cities.
7. **True or False?** Most Roman roads were built straight, avoiding sharp turns and steep hills, to make travel faster and easier.
8. **True or False?** The construction of aqueducts allowed Roman cities to grow larger and more populous by providing fresh water.
9. **True or False?** The Appian Way, one of the earliest Roman roads, connected Rome to the ancient city of Carthage.
10. **True or False?** Some Roman aqueducts are still in use today, over 2,000 years after they were built.

Answers

1. Roman roads were originally built just for military purposes.

Answer: True

- The first Roman roads were indeed constructed with military purposes in mind, allowing the Roman legions to move quickly across the empire. However, as the empire expanded, the roads became essential for trade, communication, and travel, benefiting civilians as well.

2. The famous saying "All roads lead to Rome" reflects the vast network of Roman roads that connected the empire.

Answer: True

- Roman roads radiated outward from the capital, Rome, connecting the farthest reaches of the empire. The saying "All roads lead to Rome" captures the idea that these roads were key to Rome's control and cohesion over such a large territory.

3. Roman roads were typically made of cobblestones, sand, and clay, and were not very durable.

Answer: False

- Roman roads were meticulously built using several layers of materials, including stone slabs, gravel, and sand. Their durability was legendary, and many Roman roads lasted for centuries—some even form the foundation of modern roads today.

4. Aqueducts were solely built to carry drinking water to Roman cities.

Answer: False

- While aqueducts did carry drinking water, they also supplied water for baths, fountains, irrigation, and even to power mills. Roman aqueducts were an engineering marvel that provided a wide range of uses for the cities they served.

5. The Pont du Gard in France is one of the most famous examples of a Roman aqueduct still standing today.

Answer: True

- The Pont du Gard, located in southern France, is a stunning three-tiered aqueduct bridge that dates back to the 1st century AD. It's one of the best-preserved examples of Roman engineering and remains a popular tourist destination.

6. Roman engineers developed a system to purify the water carried by aqueducts before it reached the cities.

Answer: False

- The Romans didn't use purification systems like we do today. They relied on the natural filtering of water through sediments and chose sources that were clean and safe to drink, but the water wasn't treated for bacteria or other contaminants.

7. Most Roman roads were built straight, avoiding sharp turns and steep hills, to make travel faster and easier.

Answer: True

- Roman engineers aimed to build roads as straight as possible, preferring to cut through obstacles like hills or forests rather than curve around them. This made travel faster and more efficient for both the military and traders.

8. The construction of aqueducts allowed Roman cities to grow larger and more populous by providing fresh water.

Answer: True

- By providing a reliable supply of fresh water, Roman aqueducts supported the growth of large cities, making it possible for densely populated areas to thrive. The abundance of water was crucial for public health, sanitation, and economic prosperity.

9. The Appian Way, one of the earliest Roman roads, connected Rome to the ancient city of Carthage.

Answer: False

- The Appian Way connected Rome to Brindisi, in southeastern Italy, not Carthage. It was one of the most important roads for military and trade purposes in the Roman Empire.

10. Some Roman aqueducts are still in use today, over 2,000 years after they were built.

Answer: True

- Incredibly, parts of Roman aqueducts are still in use today, particularly in cities like Segovia in Spain. Though modern infrastructure has replaced most of them, the Romans' engineering legacy remains visible and functional in some places.

The Roman Senate

Roles, Powers, and Famous Senators Quiz

1. What was the main role of the Roman Senate during the Roman Republic?

    a) Making laws
    b) Serving as an advisory body
    c) Electing the emperor
    d) Declaring war

2. Who could originally become a member of the Roman Senate?

    a) Any Roman citizen
    b) Plebeians only
    c) Patricians only
    d) Slaves after gaining freedom

3. During the Roman Republic, which office did senators typically hold before entering the Senate?

    a) Tribune
    b) Praetor
    c) Consul
    d) Aedile

4. True or False: The Roman Senate had absolute authority over all military decisions.

5. Which Roman senator famously opposed Julius Caesar and played a key role in his assassination?

    a) Pompey
    b) Cato the Younger
    c) Cicero
    d) Brutus

6. What was the *Cursus Honorum*?

   a) A series of public offices that Roman senators had to hold
   b) A special law passed by the Senate
   c) The bodyguard unit of the Senate
   d) The tax levied on senators

7. True or False: During the Roman Empire, the Senate's influence significantly diminished compared to the Republic.

8. Which famous Roman senator was known for ending his speeches with "Carthage must be destroyed" (*Carthago delenda est*)?

   a) Scipio Africanus
   b) Cicero
   c) Cato the Elder
   d) Marcus Antonius

9. Who was the Roman senator that famously spoke out against Mark Antony and was executed for it during the Second Triumvirate?

   a) Cato the Younger
   b) Cicero
   c) Octavian
   d) Agrippa

10. What was the Senate's role in the process of declaring someone an enemy of the state (*hostis publicus*)?

    a) The Senate decided by vote
    b) The emperor made the decision alone
    c) Only the people could declare it
    d) The army declared it after a battle

Answers

1. What was the main role of the Roman Senate during the Roman Republic?

Answer: b) Serving as an advisory body

- The Roman Senate acted as an advisory council to Rome's magistrates. While it didn't pass laws, it held significant sway over decisions, especially regarding foreign policy and finance, making it highly influential.

2. Who could originally become a member of the Roman Senate?

Answer: c) Patricians only

- In the early days of the Roman Republic, only patricians—members of Rome's aristocratic families—could serve in the Senate. Over time, plebeians (commoners) gained more political power and access to Senate positions.

3. During the Roman Republic, which office did senators typically hold before entering the Senate?

Answer: c) Consul

- The *Cursus Honorum* (course of honors) was the hierarchy of public offices in Rome. To enter the Senate, one typically had to hold important offices like consul, praetor, or censor, making it a career milestone for politicians.

4. True or False: The Roman Senate had absolute authority over all military decisions.

Answer: False

- The Senate advised on military matters and could allocate funds for war, but military commands were usually in the hands of consuls or, later, emperors. During times of war, decisions often bypassed the Senate.

5. Which Roman senator famously opposed Julius Caesar and played a key role in his assassination?

Answer: d) Brutus

- Marcus Junius Brutus was one of the leading senators involved in Julius Caesar's assassination on the Ides of March in 44 BC. Despite having once been close to Caesar, Brutus believed Caesar's growing power threatened the Republic.

6. What was the *Cursus Honorum*?

Answer: a) A series of public offices that Roman senators had to hold

- The *Cursus Honorum* was the sequential order of public offices, starting from lower-ranking positions and moving up to higher ones, like praetor or consul. This was the typical path for Roman politicians before entering the Senate.

7. True or False: During the Roman Empire, the Senate's influence significantly diminished compared to the Republic.

Answer: True

- Under the emperors, especially starting with Augustus, the Senate's power was reduced. While it retained some influence over ceremonial and legislative matters, the real power shifted to the emperor and his advisors.

8. Which famous Roman senator was known for ending his speeches with "Carthage must be destroyed" (*Carthago delenda est*)?

Answer: C) Cato the Elder

- Cato the Elder was a fierce opponent of Carthage and famously ended every Senate speech, regardless of topic, with "Carthage must be destroyed." This phrase emphasized his determination to see Rome's great rival defeated, leading to the Third Punic War.

9. Who was the Roman senator that famously spoke out against Mark Antony and was executed for it during the Second Triumvirate?

Answer: B) Cicero

- Cicero was a renowned orator and senator who publicly opposed Mark Antony in a series of speeches called the Philippics. After the formation of the Second Triumvirate, Antony had Cicero executed as a political enemy in 43 BC.

10. What was the Senate's role in the process of declaring someone an enemy of the state (*hostis publicus*)?

Answer: A) The Senate decided by vote

- The Senate had the power to declare a person *hostis publicus*, marking them as an enemy of Rome. This usually followed a betrayal or an illegal seizure of power, and such a declaration often led to civil war or execution.

The Fall of Rome

Key Events and Figures Quiz - Questions:

1. Which event is often considered the start of the decline of the Roman Empire?

    a) Julius Caesar's assassination
    b) The Battle of Actium
    c) The Crisis of the Third Century
    d) The rise of Christianity

2. Who was the last Roman emperor to rule over both the eastern and western halves of the Roman Empire?

    a) Constantine the Great
    b) Diocletian
    c) Theodosius I
    d) Romulus Augustulus

3. True or False: The sacking of Rome by the Visigoths in 410 AD was the first time the city had fallen to a foreign enemy in nearly 800 years.

4. Which emperor split the Roman Empire into East and West in an attempt to make it more manageable?

    a) Constantine the Great
    b) Diocletian
    c) Hadrian
    d) Nero

5. Who was the leader of the Huns, whose invasions contributed to the destabilization of the Roman Empire in the 5th century?

    a) Alaric
    b) Attila

- c) Odoacer
- d) Genseric

6. In what year did the Western Roman Empire officially fall?

- a) 395 AD
- b) 410 AD
- c) 476 AD
- d) 1453 AD

7. True or False: The Eastern Roman Empire, also known as the Byzantine Empire, continued to thrive for nearly 1,000 years after the fall of the Western Roman Empire.

8. Which barbarian king deposed the last Western Roman emperor, Romulus Augustulus, in 476 AD?

- a) Alaric
- b) Odoacer
- c) Theodoric
- d) Gaiseric

9. What role did internal corruption and political instability play in the fall of the Roman Empire?

- a) Little to no effect
- b) Significant factor
- c) Only affected the Eastern Roman Empire
- d) Only a minor role

10. Which significant Roman figure made Christianity the official religion of the Roman Empire, contributing to cultural and religious shifts?

- a) Julius Caesar
- b) Nero
- c) Constantine the Great
- d) Trajan

Answers

1. Which event is often considered the start of the decline of the Roman Empire?

Answer: c) The Crisis of the Third Century

- The Crisis of the Third Century (235–284 AD) was marked by civil war, economic collapse, and external invasions. It's often considered the start of the long decline of the Roman Empire, as the empire faced near-constant instability during this period.

2. Who was the last Roman emperor to rule over both the eastern and western halves of the Roman Empire?

Answer: c) Theodosius I

- Theodosius I was the last emperor to rule over both the eastern and western parts of the Roman Empire before it was permanently divided. After his death in 395 AD, the empire was split between his two sons, with the East becoming more dominant.

3. True or False: The sacking of Rome by the Visigoths in 410 AD was the first time the city had fallen to a foreign enemy in nearly 800 years.

Answer: True

- When Alaric and his Visigoth forces sacked Rome in 410 AD, it marked the first time in nearly 800 years that the city had fallen to a foreign power. This event was symbolic of Rome's weakening grip on its vast empire.

4. Which emperor split the Roman Empire into East and West in an attempt to make it more manageable?

Answer: b) Diocletian

- In 285 AD, Emperor Diocletian divided the Roman Empire into the Western and Eastern halves, each ruled by its own emperor, in an effort to make the vast empire more manageable and defendable. This division, however, would later contribute to the empire's downfall.

5. Who was the leader of the Huns, whose invasions contributed to the destabilization of the Roman Empire in the 5th century?

Answer: b) Attila

- Attila the Hun, known as the "Scourge of God," led devastating invasions into both the Eastern and Western Roman Empires during the 5th century, further weakening Rome's defenses and contributing to the empire's collapse.

6. In what year did the Western Roman Empire officially fall?

Answer: c) 476 AD

- The Western Roman Empire officially fell in 476 AD when the barbarian king Odoacer deposed the last Roman emperor, Romulus Augustulus. This event is traditionally considered the end of the ancient Roman Empire in the West.

7. True or False: The Eastern Roman Empire, also known as the Byzantine Empire, continued to thrive for nearly 1,000 years after the fall of the Western Roman Empire.

Answer: True

- While the Western Roman Empire fell in 476 AD, the Eastern Roman Empire, also called the Byzantine Empire, continued to thrive until 1453 AD, when Constantinople fell to the Ottoman Turks.

8. Which barbarian king deposed the last Western Roman emperor, Romulus Augustulus, in 476 AD?

Answer: b) Odoacer

- Odoacer, a Germanic barbarian leader, deposed Romulus Augustulus in 476 AD, effectively bringing an end to the

Western Roman Empire. Odoacer declared himself ruler of Italy but did not claim the title of emperor.

9. What role did internal corruption and political instability play in the fall of the Roman Empire?

Answer: b) Significant factor

- Internal corruption, political instability, and frequent power struggles between generals and emperors significantly weakened the Roman Empire. These issues led to inefficiency, economic troubles, and an inability to manage the empire's vast territories effectively.

10. Which significant Roman figure made Christianity the official religion of the Roman Empire, contributing to cultural and religious shifts?

Answer: c) Constantine the Great

- Constantine the Great, in the early 4th century AD, played a crucial role in the spread of Christianity by making it the dominant religion of the Roman Empire. This shift had profound effects on Roman culture, politics, and society as the empire transitioned away from its traditional pagan beliefs.

Roman Religion

Rituals, Temples, and Practices Quiz - Questions:

1. What was the primary role of the Pontifex Maximus in Roman religion?

    a) Leading military expeditions
    b) Serving as the head priest of the Roman state
    c) Overseeing the Senate
    d) Performing sacrifices to Jupiter alone

2. Which Roman goddess was considered the protector of the hearth and home, with a temple where an eternal flame burned in her honor?

    a) Minerva
    b) Vesta
    c) Venus
    d) Juno

3. True or False: Roman priests, known as augurs, interpreted the will of the gods by observing the flight of birds.

4. The Roman festival of Saturnalia, celebrated in December, honored which god, and influenced which modern holiday?

    a) Mars, and influenced Veterans Day
    b) Saturn, and influenced Christmas
    c) Jupiter, and influenced Easter
    d) Neptune, and influenced Halloween

5. Which of the following was considered the most sacred site in Rome, home to the famous Temple of Jupiter?

    a) Palatine Hill
    b) Aventine Hill

- c) Capitoline Hill
- d) Quirinal Hill

6. What was the primary purpose of a *sacrifice* in Roman religious practices?

- a) To gain favor with the gods
- b) To punish criminals
- c) To settle disputes between citizens
- d) To commemorate fallen soldiers

7. True or False: The Vestal Virgins, who guarded the sacred fire of Vesta, were women chosen from prominent families and served for life.

8. Which Roman god of war was considered the father of Romulus and Remus, the legendary founders of Rome?

- a) Mars
- b) Mercury
- c) Apollo
- d) Pluto

9. What was a *haruspex* responsible for in Roman religion?

- a) Overseeing public festivals
- b) Interpreting the will of the gods by examining animal entrails
- c) Managing temple finances
- d) Prophesizing future military victories through dreams

10. Which emperor made Christianity the official religion of the Roman Empire, marking the end of traditional Roman religious practices?

- a) Nero
- b) Constantine the Great
- c) Augustus
- d) Hadrian

Answers

1. What was the primary role of the Pontifex Maximus in Roman religion?

Answer: b) Serving as the head priest of the Roman state

- The Pontifex Maximus was the chief priest in Rome, responsible for overseeing religious ceremonies, maintaining temples, and managing the priesthood. This position later became a symbol of great political power, and Roman emperors eventually held the title.

2. Which Roman goddess was considered the protector of the hearth and home, with a temple where an eternal flame burned in her honor?

Answer: B) Vesta

- Vesta was the goddess of the hearth, and her temple in Rome housed the sacred flame that symbolized the eternal protection of the city. The Vestal Virgins maintained this flame and performed rituals to honor her.

3. True or False: Roman priests, known as augurs, interpreted the will of the gods by observing the flight of birds.

Answer: True

- Augurs were priests who specialized in interpreting the will of the gods by studying the flight patterns of birds. This practice, known as augury, was used to determine the favorability of actions, particularly for military and political decisions.

4. The Roman festival of Saturnalia, celebrated in December, honored which god, and influenced which modern holiday?

Answer: B) Saturn, and influenced Christmas

- Saturnalia was a week-long festival celebrating Saturn, the god of agriculture. The festival involved feasting, gift-giving, and a temporary reversal of social roles. Many of these traditions influenced the later development of Christmas celebrations.

5. Which of the following was considered the most sacred site in Rome, home to the famous Temple of Jupiter?

Answer: C) Capitoline Hill

- Capitoline Hill was one of Rome's most important religious sites, home to the Temple of Jupiter Optimus Maximus, the chief deity of the Roman pantheon. The hill was a central hub for religious and political activities.

6. What was the primary purpose of a *sacrifice* in Roman religious practices?

Answer: A) To gain favor with the gods

- Sacrifices, often involving animals like sheep or bulls, were a crucial part of Roman religious rituals. They were offered to gain the favor of the gods, seek blessings, or avert disaster, especially before important events like battles.

7. True or False: The Vestal Virgins, who guarded the sacred fire of Vesta, were women chosen from prominent families and served for life.

Answer: False

- While Vestal Virgins were indeed chosen from noble families and served long terms, their service lasted 30 years, not for life. After completing their service, they could marry, though many chose not to.

8. Which Roman god of war was considered the father of Romulus and Remus, the legendary founders of Rome?

Answer: A) Mars

- Mars, the Roman god of war, was regarded as the father of Romulus and Remus, the mythological twin brothers who founded Rome. Mars was an important deity, symbolizing military power and the protection of Rome.

9. What was a *haruspex* responsible for in Roman religion?

Answer: B) Interpreting the will of the gods by examining animal entrails

- A *haruspex* was a religious figure who performed divination by inspecting the entrails of sacrificed animals, especially the liver, to interpret omens and determine the favor of the gods.

10. Which emperor made Christianity the official religion of the Roman Empire, marking the end of traditional Roman religious practices?

Answer: B) Constantine the Great

- In 313 AD, Constantine issued the Edict of Milan, granting religious tolerance to Christians. Later, under Theodosius I, Christianity became the official religion of the empire, signaling the end of the traditional Roman pantheon.

The Life of Livia Drusilla

The Powerful and Influential Wife of Augustus

Livia Drusilla—Rome's original power broker. While Augustus, the first Roman emperor, took center stage in the grand political theater of Rome, Livia was always in the background, pulling strings, influencing decisions, and making sure her family's legacy stayed intact. Think of her as the ultimate Roman matriarch, capable of wielding power with a grace that would make modern political strategists jealous.

Born in 58 BC to a wealthy and prominent Roman family, Livia's life started out with the usual expectations for a Roman noblewoman: marriage, children, and some light household management. But fate had grander plans for her. After a brief marriage to her first husband, Tiberius Claudius Nero (with whom she had two sons, including the future emperor Tiberius), Livia caught the eye of a rising political star—Gaius Octavius, who would later become Augustus.

Livia was already pregnant with her second son when Augustus (still Octavian at the time) set his sights on her. Divorce was swiftly arranged, and Livia married Augustus in 38 BC. It wasn't your typical Roman love story, but this was a power couple for the ages. From then on, Livia wasn't just a wife; she was Augustus's most trusted advisor, known for her sharp intellect, political acumen, and ability to navigate the complex Roman court.

Livia had a reputation for being deeply involved in the affairs of state, though she maintained a public image of modesty and humility. She played the game of power brilliantly, ensuring that her sons, particularly Tiberius, stayed in Augustus's good graces. And if whispers of darker deeds—like the alleged poisoning of rivals—circulated around her, well, that just added to her mystique.

Rome's elite didn't mess with Livia, because Livia always seemed to get her way.

When Augustus died in AD 14, it was Tiberius who succeeded him, largely thanks to Livia's maneuvering. But her influence didn't stop there. As the mother of the emperor, Livia continued to play a significant role in shaping Roman politics and ensuring that the Julio-Claudian dynasty thrived. She lived to the ripe old age of 86, outlasting many of her contemporaries, and was deified by her grandson, the emperor Claudius.

Livia Drusilla was a master of quiet power—a woman who, without holding official political office, had more sway than most men in the empire. Her life is a testament to how, even in a patriarchal society, women could find ways to influence the course of history from behind the scenes.

The Decline and Fall of the Western Empire

The Final Days of Rome and Its Enduring Legacy

If you think Rome's fall was like a grand, explosive finale, think again. The decline of the Western Roman Empire was less a cataclysmic event and more a slow-motion unraveling. Picture a mighty ship that's been weathering storms for centuries, finally succumbing to leaks and rot, while its sailors desperately patch holes. By the time the ship goes under, most of the crew has already abandoned ship—or switched to the Eastern Roman (Byzantine) fleet.

The Western Roman Empire officially fell in 476 AD, but the cracks had been showing long before. It all started with internal issues: corruption, political instability, economic troubles, and a bloated, overstretched military. For centuries, the empire had grown too large, too unwieldy, and by the time of the 3rd and 4th centuries, managing such a vast territory became impossible. Emperors came and went at a dizzying pace, often assassinated by their own troops or rivals. It was a dangerous game, being emperor of Rome.

But the fall wasn't just an internal affair. The empire's borders were under constant pressure from outside forces—Germanic tribes, Huns, and even Persians. By the 5th century, barbarian incursions had become invasions. Rome, which had once expanded effortlessly across Europe, Africa, and Asia, was now on the defensive. The Visigoths famously sacked Rome in 410 AD, a symbolic moment that signaled the empire's vulnerability. But it wasn't the last blow.

The real knockout punch came in 476 AD when the barbarian king Odoacer deposed the last Roman emperor in the West, the young and relatively powerless Romulus Augustulus. And just like that, the Western Roman Empire was no more—at least in name. The Eastern Roman Empire (Byzantine Empire) continued to thrive for another thousand years, but Rome itself had fallen.

Yet, the end of the Western Roman Empire wasn't the end of its influence. Far from it. The legacy of Rome—its laws, its culture, its art, and its governance—lived on in the very barbarians who conquered it. The so-called "barbarian" rulers adopted Roman customs, converted to Christianity (the religion that Rome had officially embraced before its fall), and in many ways, tried to preserve the Roman way of life. The very title of "emperor" would resurface in various forms throughout European history, from Charlemagne's Holy Roman Empire to Napoleon's ambitions.

Rome's infrastructure—its roads, aqueducts, and monumental buildings—continued to serve new generations. And let's not forget the Latin language, which evolved into the Romance languages spoken by millions today. Even modern legal systems owe a debt to Roman law.

So, while the Western Roman Empire may have officially ended, its impact endured. Rome's fall was not so much an end, but the beginning of a new chapter in European history. Its legacy, woven into the fabric of Western civilization, lives on in the languages, laws, and institutions that define much of the modern world.

Final Thoughts

Marching Into the Future

Congratulations, traveler of time! You've ventured through the triumphs and trials of the Roman Empire, from the bustling streets of ancient Rome to the heart of the Senate and the sands of the Colosseum. We hope this journey has been as thrilling for you as it was for the legions marching into battle—though with far fewer spears and sandals involved.

But the adventure doesn't end here! If you've enjoyed this deep dive into Roman history and trivia, there's more waiting for you. Simply **scan the QR code** below for exclusive access to free trivia content that will test your newfound knowledge and keep the fun going. And hey, if this book made you laugh, think, or say "Wow, I didn't know that," we'd love to hear about it. Leaving a **review on Amazon** helps other history buffs join in on the excitement, and we'd greatly appreciate your feedback.

So, tighten your sandals one last time, look to the horizon, and remember—history is best enjoyed when shared. May the wisdom of Rome stay with you, and may your future trivia quests be ever victorious!

Printed in Great Britain
by Amazon